ACKNOWLEDGMENTS

This magazine has been published by Wharncliffe History Magazines in association with Pen and Sword Military Books Limited, with the purpose of creating an awareness and an interest, not only in the sixty-fifth anniversary of the Dambuster raid but also in the subject of aviation history.

For over twenty years Pen and Sword has published numerous military, naval and aviation books covering various conflicts throughout history. A vast amount of aviation titles have been published over the past few years, covering the personal accounts of airmen who have taken part in many conflicts, stretching from the First World War through to the war in Iraq. Other titles include the design and development of Britain's much loved aircraft such as the Jaguar, Lightning, Swift, Victor and the Joint Strike Fighter, just to name a few, all of which are packed with photographs and supported with colour profiles illustrated by Dave Windle.

These publications would not have been possible if it had not been for the skill and dedication of the authors, who have painstakingly researched and written about these subjects in order to bring them to light.

Extracts have been taken from some of these titles to produce this magazine. Much more information can be gleaned from reading the books on these subjects, details of which are mentioned at the end of each chapter. Pen and Sword have added more colour illustrations and images to the text in order to add more for the reader, making this a very special anniversary publication.

Pen and Sword Military Books would like to thank; Ken Delve, Charles Foster, Arthur G Thorning, Susan Ottaway, Chris Ward and Andreas Wachtel, whose works have appeared in this magazine DAMBUSTERS: THE RAID SIXTY-FIVE YEARS ON.

Wharncliffe

HISTORY MAGAZINES

in association with

PEN & SWORD MILITARY BOOKS LTD.

If you would like to place an advertisement in any of our publications please contact;

CAROLYN MILLS

ADVERTISING MANAGER

TELEPHONE: 01226 734704

FAX: 01226 734703

E-mail: carolynm@whmagazines.co.uk

THE DRILL HALL • EASTGATE • BARNSLEY • SOUTH YORKSHIRE • S70 2EU

VISIT THE WEBSITE NOW:

www.pen-and-sword.co.uk/dambusters

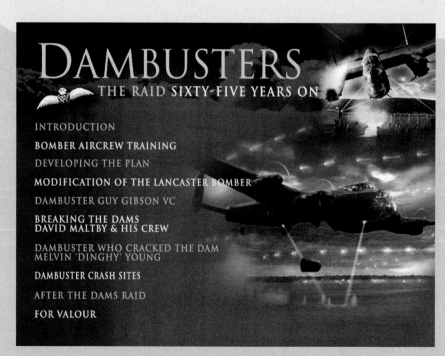

DAMBUSTERS
THE RAID SIXTY-FIVE YEARS ON

INTRODUCTION

BOMBER AIRCREW TRAINING

DEVELOPING THE PLAN

MODIFICATION OF THE LANCASTER BOMBER

DAMBUSTER GUY GIBSON VC

BREAKING THE DAMS
DAVID MALTBY & HIS CREW

DAMBUSTER WHO CRACKED THE DAM
MELVIN 'DINGHY' YOUNG

DAMBUSTER CRASH SITES

AFTER THE DAMS RAID

FOR VALOUR

Wharncliffe
HISTORY MAGAZINES

In association with;

Pen & Sword Military Books.

First published in Great Britain in 2008 by
Wharncliffe History Magazines
47 Church Street
Barnsley
South Yorkshire
S70 2AS

Copyright © Wharncliffe Publishing, 2008

Edited by Rebecca Lawther

Design, layout, maps & photograph colouring:
Jon Wilkinson

ISBN: 978 184415 800 3

A CIP catalogue record for this book is
available from the British Library.

Printed and bound in the United Kingdom

For a complete list of Pen & Sword titles please
contact
PEN & SWORD BOOKS LIMITED
47 Church Street, Barnsley, South Yorkshire,
S70 2AS, England
E-mail: enquiries@pen-and-sword.co.uk
Website: www.pen-and-sword.co.uk

CONTENTS

INTRODUCTION

Operation *Chastise*, the legendary raid on the dams of Germany's industrial Ruhr region, was one of epic proportions. It demonstrated originality, fearlessness and courage on behalf of those who calculated the breach of the Dams, and those who carried out the raid.

Germany's industrial heartland was identified by the Air Ministry as an important strategic target prior to the war. With the dams chosen as targets, due to the effect their destruction would have on the water supply for industry, cities and canals, the methods by which they could be attacked had to be carefully considered.

Barnes Wallis, an aircraft designer for Vickers-Armstrong, designed a weapon with the dams specifically in mind. This cylindrical bomb – codenamed 'Upkeep' – was to be dropped, spinning rapidly backwards, from a low altitude at the right speed which would allow it to bounce over the surface of the water. The Avro Lancaster aircraft, which were used for the raid, were specially adapted to carry the 'bouncing bombs'.

The mission was carried out by the specially formed No 617 Squadron which was led by Wing Commander Guy Gibson. Gibson was involved in the selection of pilots and crew, and was awarded the Victoria Cross for his heroism. Most of the crew were not briefed on the details of the operation until 16 May, just hours before they were due to fly.

This magazine looks at the training of the aircrew of Bomber Command, some of whom would later form No 617 Squadron; the formation and development of the plan for the raid on the dams; how the weapon was designed and tested, and how the Lancaster was adapted to carry the weapon. The magazine also focuses on several of the pilots and their crews who took part in the raid, including some of those who did not make it back.

The success of the Dambuster raids has been somewhat debated in the years since they took place: although the bombs fulfiled their purpose and two of the dams were successfully breached, the attack was costly in lives and did not have the long-term effects that had been hoped on the Ruhr's industrial output. However, as described in the latter chapters of this magazine, it did have enormous propaganda value for the Allies.

GLOSSARY

*	(medal) and Bar	LAC	Leading aircraftman/woman
10/10ths	Complete cloud cover	LMF	Lack of Moral Fibre
AA	Anti-Aircraft	LNSF	Light Night Striking Force
AAA	Anti-Aircraft Artillery	Loran	Long-Range Navigation
Ack-ack	Flak, anti-aircraft fire	M/T	Motor Transport
ADGB	Air Defence of Great Britain	Mae West	Life Jacket, named after American actress
Adj	Adjutant	Mandrel	100 Group airborne radar jamming device
AFC	Air Force Cross	MC	Medium Capacity bomb
AOC	Air Officer Commanding	MCU	Mosquito Conversion Unit
ASR	Air Sea Rescue	Mess	Possibly from the Latin mensa (table) or Old
ATS	Air Training Squadron		French mes (dish of food)
Batman	From the French *bat*, meaning pack saddle.	Met	Meteorological
	A male or female mess steward responsible	Mickey Mouse	Bomb aiming equipment
	for an officer's well being on base	Milk Run	Regular run of operations to a particular
BBC	British Broadcasting Corporation		target (US, easy mission)
BFTS	British Flying Training School	Millennium	One of three 1,000 bomber raids on
Big City	Berlin		German cities, May to June 1942
Brevet	Flying Badge	Monica	British tail warning radar device
BSDU	Bomber Support Development Unit	MTU	Mosquito Training Unit
CO	Commanding Officer	NCO	Non-Commissioned Officer
CoG	Centre of Gravity	Newhave	Flares dropped by PFF
Cookie	4,000lb bomb	Nickels	Propaganda leaflets
CRT	Cathode Ray Tube	Night Ranger	Operation to engage air and ground targets
C-scope	CRT showing frontal elevation of target		within a wide but specified area, by night
Day Ranger	Operation to engage air and ground targets	Oboe	Ground-controlled radar system of blind
	within a wide but specified area, by day		bombing, in which one station indicated the
DCM	Distinguished Conduct Medal		track to be followed and another the bomb
DFC	Distinguished Flying Cross		release point
DFM	Distinguished Flying Medal	Ops	Operations
Drem lighting	System of outer markers and runway	OT	Operational Training
	approach lights	Other ranks	Ranks other than commissioned officers
DSC	Distinguished Service Cross	OTU	Operational Training Unit
DSO	Distinguished Service Order	Paramatta	Flares dropped by PFF
e/a	Enemy Aircraft	PFF	Pathfinder Force
ETA	Estimated time of arrival	PoW	Prisoner of war
FIDO	Fog Investigation and Dispersal Operation	PR	Photographic Reconnaissance
Flak	German term for anti-aircraft fire	PRU	Photographic Reconnaissance Unit
Flight offices	Usually occupied by the CO, flight	R/T	Radio Telephony
	commanders and their slaves	RAAF	Royal Australian Air Force
Flight	Flight sergeant	RAE	Royal Aircraft Establishment
FNSF	Fast Night Striking Force	RAFVR	Royal Air Force Volunteer Reserve
Freelance	Patrol with the objective of picking up a	RCAF	Royal Canadian Air Force
	chance or visual of the enemy	RCM	Radio countermeasure
Gardening	Minelaying	RNZAF	Royal New Zealand Air Force
Gee	British medium-range navigational aid using	RP	Rocket Projectile
	ground transmitters and an airborne	SASO	Senior Air Staff Officer
	receiver	SD	Special Duties
GP	General Purpose bomb	SEAC	South East Asia Command
Gremlin	A mythical mischievous creature invented	Serrate	British equipment designed to home on
	by the RAF		Lichtenstein AI radar
H2S	British 10cm experimental airborne radar	Sortie	Operational flight by a single aircraft
	navigational and target location	TI	Target Indicator
HE	High Explosive (bomb)	TNT	TriNitro Toluene
HEI	High Explosive Incendiary	U/S	Unserviceable
HRH	His Royal Highness	UHF	Ultra-High Frequency
IAS	Indicated Air Speed	W/T	Wireless telephony
IFF	Identification friend or foe	WAAF	Women's Auxiliary Air Force (member of)
Intruder	Offensive night operation to fixed point or	WOP/AG	Wireless operator/air gunner
	specified target	Y-Service	British organisation monitoring German
IO	Intelligence Officer		radio transmissions to and from aircraft

THE
DAMBUSTER
OBJECTIVES
1943

A map showing the airfields used by 617 Squadron and the German dams

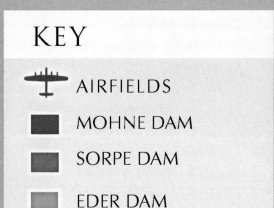

KEY

✈ AIRFIELDS

◼ MOHNE DAM

◼ SORPE DAM

◼ EDER DAM

NO

YORKSHIRE

LINCOLNSHIRE

SCAMPTON

✈ WADDINGTON

✈ WOODHALL

✈ CONNINGSBY

NORFOLK

ENGLAND

ENGLISH CHANNEL

FRAN

DENMARK

BALTIC SEA

TH SEA

NETHERLANDS

GERMANY

GREVEN

MUNSTER

ESSEN

HAMM

SOEST

DUSSELDORF

River Ruhr

Dortmund

Ruthen

River Mohne

KASSEL

BELGIUM

Rhine

River Eder

COLOGNE

9

'Once a pilot has mastered the new type, he has to be trained in advanced instrument flying, and long-distance flying by day and night, but to enable him to do this the rest of the crew must have reached a satisfactory standard in wireless and navigation. Finally, the complete crew must be taught bombing and air firing.'

BOMBER AIRCREW TRAINING

'It can be justly asserted that the success of the Bomber Offensive depended ultimately on the standard of training which could be maintained. It would have been easy to improve training at the expense of the front line by increasing the length of the courses given; by training Lancaster crews on Lancasters only; by ensuring that all the best aircrews were taken off operations early in order to fill the pressing need for instructor posts, and by introducing new equipment into the training units first, so that crews could have been provided fully trained in all new devices. It is believed that the best all-round result was obtained.'

AIR MARSHAL ARTHUR HARRIS IN HIS DESPATCH ON BOMBER OPERATIONS

By Ken Delve

This article was extracted from Ken Delve's book *Bomber Command 1936-1968 – An Operational & Historical Record* and is reproduced here by permission of Pen and Sword Books Ltd.

In this chapter the focus will be on the later stages of bomber aircrew training, from the Operational Training Unit onwards, with little mention of selection or early stages of training such as Elementary Flying Training School (EFTS) and Service Flying Training School (SFTS). By the time that aircrew had reached OTU they were already trained in their specialisation and the aim of the subsequent stages was to provide them with training on more appropriate types and with an emphasis on operationally-related activities – as well as building the crew cooperation skills that were vital to a multi-crew bomber.

THE EARLY YEARS

In 1938 Air Chief Marshal (ACM) Ludlow-Hewitt, AOC-in-C Bomber Command, pointed out that,

'One of the chief results of this year's experience is that the work of the members of a modern bomber [by which he meant the Wellington] requires a very much higher standing and specialisation than has hitherto been contemplated.'

This was followed up by a proposal from one of his staff, Air Marshal Welsh in November for the establishment of one Advanced Flying Training Centre for each operational Group to:

'Provide each one with a reservoir or pool from which replacement crews can be drawn and to train the output of the Flying Training Schools up to an operational standard before it passes to the operational squadrons.'

Thus was born the idea of additional training for qualified aircrew to make them better suited for front-line duties. In this chapter we are going to focus on this

Air Marshal Arthur Harris also known as 'Bomber Harris'.

stage of training, from the arrival of the aircrew member into the Bomber Command training machine until his departure to join a squadron.

It was considered that six of the new Group Pool Squadrons would be able to feed the seventy-three operational squadrons, and as an interim measure a number of the non-mobilizable squadrons from the Bomber Command Order of Battle would take on this role. From these simple beginnings, the training machine would grow to one employing over 2,000 aircraft and thousands of personnel. First to take on the role was 75 Squadron at Honington, which was still equipped with Harrows in March when it adopted the new role, although these gave way to Wellingtons in July. Indeed it was to be the Vickers-Armstrong Wellingtons that became the workhorse of the majority of the later Operational Training Units (OTUs).

By June 1939 there were nine Group Pool Squadrons, but this interim measure had its detractors. Ludlow-Hewitt commented:

'It is most uneconomical in practice, even in peacetime, to make operational squadrons undertake the initial operational training of pilots and crews coming direct from the flying schools, and it would be quite impossible in wartime. It is necessary, therefore, to consider the extent of the training organisation required to undertake the whole of this initial operational training.'

At this stage the pre-squadron training course was

Wellington bomber in flight.

notionally fourteen weeks long and included sixty-two flying hours, and it was suggested that a twenty-four-aircraft unit would be able to train twenty-two pilots per course. On 16 September 1939, it was agreed that the Group Pool squadrons would be concentrated into a separate training group, No 6 Group, under Air Commodore Macneece-Foster.

Bomber Command had decided to allocate one operational type to each operational Group, the Wellingtons being concentrated in No 3 Group, and this was reflected in the establishment and syllabus of the appropriate training unit(s). In the case of the Wellington units, three squadrons had been transferred to No 6 Group – 75 and 148 Squadrons at Harwell and 215 Squadron in Bassingbourn. Each unit was given an establishment of twelve aircraft, half of which were Ansons, although the latter were in short supply at this time and it was more usual for only three or four to be on strength per unit. The course included fifty-five flying hours and there were eleven crews per course. In the light of early operational experience a major change was proposed at the end of 1939 and this led to the creation of the Operational Training Unit. The initial part of the process was to bring together two squadrons at each of the training airfields, although this ideal was not always achieved. The final part of the process was implemented in spring 1940 by the simple expedient of combining Pool Squadrons and re-designating them as Operational Training Units within a new numbering system.

In February Ludlow-Hewitt had defined the role of the new training units:

'The proper role of the OTU is to convert otherwise fully-trained pilots, air observers

Bristol Blenheim.

Handley Page Hampdens. Its bomb-load had major limitations but it was to remain in service until late 1942.

and air gunners to the type of aircraft in which they will be required to operate and to give them sufficient operational training to fit them to take their place in operational squadrons. Obviously the first essential is to teach the new pilots how to fly a service type by day and night, which entails a considerable amount of local flying. Once a pilot has mastered the new type, he has to be trained in advanced instrument flying, and long-distance flying by day and night, but to enable him to do this the rest of the crew must have reached a satisfactory standard in wireless and navigation. Finally, the complete crew must be taught bombing and air firing.'

By April three of eight OTUs had Wellingtons, two had Blenheims and one each had Battles, Whitleys or Hampdens. Standard aircraft establishment was seventy aircraft, 25 per cent of which should be Ansons, and the courses were set at six weeks to include fifty-five flying hours. Courses comprised 180 pupils: sixty pilots, thirty observers and ninety air gunners (ie thirty crews). Each OTU was meant to have one parent and one satellite airfield. Inevitably these paper numbers were not always adhered to in the real world and numbers and split of aircraft would vary, as would the number of pupils and airfield availability.

At full output, the OTU organisation was able to provide 930 pilots a year, but Bomber Command was already predicting a need for 1,350 pilots. It is worth remembering that at this time each operational bomber had two pilots, and when OTU output is discussed it is usually crews rather than pilots that are referred to.

However, it proved constantly difficult for the training units to match crew output to the requirements of the front-line – a problem that was affected by a great many factors, not least of which was the loss rate of crews on operations. The flow of crews could only be increased by either cutting the length of the course, with a consequent reduction in quality, or increasing the size/number of OTUs. Whilst the latter might appear an obvious choice, it was a struggle to find aircraft, airfields and manpower for any expansion – at a time when the front-line was also expanding. Two more OTUs were formed in June and the following month a new training Group, No 7 Group, was formed.

On 16 July 1940, Bomber Command approved the employment of OTU aircraft on leaflet-dropping missions, although this was restricted to a limited area in France. Three aircraft took part in the first such 'attack' on the night of 18/19 July. The employment of OTU aircraft on operations became standard policy, the theory being that sending student crews to 'easy' targets was a means of increasing their experience and confidence. It was a philosophy that was to cause much argument and dissent, but one that appears to have been generally supported by the student crews, all of whom were keen to join in the offensive as soon as possible. The first loss occurred on 27/28 July when Wellington N3002 of No 11 OTU crashed at Clophill when returning from a leaflet raid; four of the crew were injured.

SHORTAGE OF CREWS

By November, the OTU course had been lengthened to

The rear view of an Armstrong-Whitworth Whitley. Although it had the capability to carry a 3,000lb bomb-load, the Whitleys were later to be used for leaflet dropping campaigns.

ten weeks with ninety flying hours, primarily because of a reduction in flying hours at the Service Flying Training School (SFTS) stage of pilot training. This had an immediate impact on output and it was decided that four more OTUs would be needed.

The changes made in the latter part of 1940 had the net effect that the training units were not able to produce enough crews for the planned expansion of the operational squadrons. Input of pilots was not expected to be a problem as the first pilots from the overseas SFTSs were starting to arrive. What was needed was an expansion of the OTU organisation itself. It was predicted that twenty such units would be required (there were ten at the end of 1940), along with 600 instructor pilots – at a time when there were only 1,120 pilots in the front-line. There was no simple solution to this apparent dichotomy of interests, other than to reduce the amount of training and thus speed up the flow of crews.

In March 1941 it was decided that as an interim measure the course would be reduced to eight weeks, with fifty-five flying hours. According to ACM Sir Charles Portal, AOC-in-C Bomber Command:

'It is of vital importance to obtain a greater output from the OTUs, since if we do not do so, I do not see how we are to produce the crews for our expansion and at the same time keep up our pressure on Germany.'

The reduced course would mean that a pilot would arrive on his squadron having flown 177 hours, comprising fifty hours at EFTS, probably on Tiger Moths, seventy-two hours at SFTS, probably on Ansons, and fifty-five at the OTU.

Although two more OTUs were formed in March, in the following month Portal agreed to further cuts in training with the proposal that: *'The course should be radically cut and that trainees should go to squadrons for a short period as second pilots'*. On 12 April the length of the course was set at thirty-two flying hours over six weeks, although this experimental system was to be trialled at a selection of OTUs before being universally adopted. Meanwhile three further units were formed, bringing the total to sixteen – nine were equipped with Wellingtons (which took up forty per cent of the Wellington strength in the UK!), whilst the others had Whitleys or Blenheims, along with training types such as Ansons.

Philip Dawson was at Wellesbourne Mountford (No. 22 OTU) in May.

'The aircraft were generally pretty clapped out having been taken from operational units. The first part of the course was general flying, circuits and bumps and familiarisation with the aircraft. The second phase was the more 'advanced' elements with navigation and bombing; the longest sorties were about five hours and often included visits to the ranges on the Isle of Man to bomb smoke floats. A crew on the course in front of us was killed in an accident

and we were 'accelerated' to join this course, this meant flying eight trips, day and night, in one twenty-four-hour period!'

The shortened course was not proving a success, especially as the front-line squadrons were unable to provide the promised 'top-up' training. In October the old eight-week course was re-introduced for all OTUs, although the Command was requesting a twelve-week duration for the winter courses to allow for poor weather.

After two full years of bombing attacks there was strong evidence that Bomber Command had reached a crisis point. However, 1942 was to see a major change in the Command's fortunes and this was reflected in the training organisation.

In February 1942 Air Vice Marshal Arthur Harris had taken over as AOC-in-C and the following month the Command undertook a number of studies into aircraft crewing, the motivation for this being the continued high loss rate. Bomber Command had lost ninety aircraft and crews in the six-week period to the end of March, which had including a number of attacks where the loss rate was around ten per cent. Inevitably there was a direct correlation between losses, the rate of expansion of the Command and the requirements from the training organisation. The studies focused on crew roles and the options for streamlining the system – in other words saving time and thus increasing the output.

However, the most significant decision was the removal of the two-pilot system that had hitherto been standard for medium/heavy bombers. Harris was also keen to maximise employment of his trained crews and overall expected two operational tours and two training tours before they could be released to any other jobs.

The change in crewing had a fundamental effect on the training syllabus, the core decisions being:

1. Only one pilot per crew to be trained.

2. Air Bomber added to crew, allowing navigator to concentrate on navigation – part of this decision was the problem of the bomb aimer keeping good night vision. The air bomber would also receive some air gunner training to man the front guns.

3. Only one Wireless Operator/Air Gunner per crew, the other being replaced by an Air Gunner with no wireless training. In the four-engined bomber two air gunners were added.

According to Harris in his Despatch on War Operations:

'These changes made it possible to give each member of the crew a full course on his own subjects, and, particularly in the case of the pilot, enabled a much better course to be given, as it was no longer necessary to give a double number of circuits and bumps to each crew. This in turn relieved both the strain on the pilot instructors and the congestion around the OTU airfields.'

The lack of a second pilot was addressed by giving one

Bombadier

Hampden gunners practising with a gun rig.

Wireless Operator

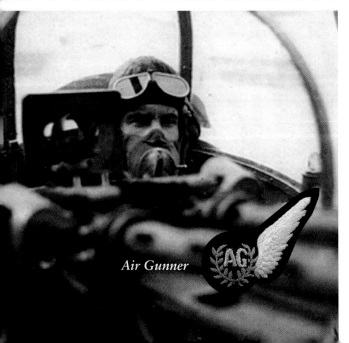

Air Gunner

of the crew members rudimentary training on the Link Trainer and in the aircraft to act as a Pilot's Assistant (PA). This role was allocated to the Air Bomber, although with the later introduction of a Flight Engineer to the heavies, he took on the PA task.

It is worth noting that the Whitley flew its last operational bombing raid on 27/28 April 1942, although OTU Whitleys continued to fly leaflet-dropping missions for some time, so the type did not vanish completely from operations.

CHOOSING A CREW

It was whilst at the OTU that crews were formed:

'Then they go to the OTU where they are formed into a crew and begin to learn team work. The duties of all members of the crew are carefully defined as far as the principal tasks are concerned, but the captain of each aircraft is responsible for arranging the duties of his crew and for seeing that they carry them out punctually and efficiently.'

A new pilot would start to trawl to find the rest of a crew, the decision being left to the individuals as far as possible rather than the 'system' just putting names together. It worked remarkably well and gradually the crew would come together.

This was outlined in the August 1944 Aircrew Training Bulletin:

'The aircrew meet for the first time at the OTU and during the first two weeks of the ground course are given certain discretion in sorting themselves out into complete crews (with the exception of the Flight Engineer who does not arrive until later.)'

John Long went through the crewing up 'process' at Moreton-in-the-Marsh (No 21 OTU):

'On arrival we were directed to one of the hangars where the completely undirected process of crewing up took place. Pilots, Navigators, Wireless Operators, Bomb Aimers

15

and Gunners all milled around, making their categories and names known to each other as the random selection went on. Having crewed up, through the rest of July and on into September we became a 'unit'. We were learning not only how to operate our war machine but also about each other.'

REORGANISATION, GROWTH & OPERATIONS

May 1942 saw a reorganisation of the training system with No 6 Group becoming No 91 Group and No 7 Group becoming No 92 Group, the main reason being that the lower numbers were being allocated to new operational Groups, although in the event only No 6 (RCAF) Group formed. This was to be a difficult year for the Command but also one in which it 'turned the corner' in terms of operational effectiveness; however, overall the Command contracted in size – with exception of the formation, in June, of a third OTU Group, No 93 Group with its HQ at Burton-on-Trent.

A young airman wearing the white cap flash indicating trainee aircrew. Right: Having qualified he now wears the Flight Engineer half brevet, showing that he is now ready for front-line operational duties. FRANK NEWMAN

At this stage of the war, it was taking an average of eighteen months for a trainee to get from 'civvy street' to a front-line squadron. After selection, the route started with three days at the local Aircrew Reception Centre (ACRC); here the main task was getting kitted out. Then came what many thought was the worst part, twelve weeks at an Initial Training Wing (ITW) which included intensive classroom work on technical and air-related subjects, but also far too much 'bull'. This was followed by flying training through elementary/basic, advanced and finally operational phases.

From 1941 the training units had been participating in operational sorties, albeit only leaflet dropping over notionally easy targets. However, the Thousand-Bomber raids of early summer 1942 would not have been possible without the widespread use of aircraft and crews from the training units. Of the 1,047 bombers tasked to attack Cologne on the night of 30/31 May, two training Groups provided 365 aircraft. No 91 Group sent 236 Wellingtons and twenty-one Whitleys, whilst No 92 Group sent sixty-three Wellingtons and forty-five Hampdens. Two further raids followed whilst this massive force was available, Essen (1/2 June) and Bremen (25/26 June). The latter was a disaster for the OTU crews, with the force of around 200 Wellingtons

and Whitleys suffering almost thirty losses, with 10, 11 and 12 OTUs each losing four aircraft. Regardless of such losses, it was not practical to keep the training units away from their primary task any longer and besides, Harris felt that he had proved the point that used en masse, the bomber weapon could be decisive. Despite the fact that the units were released from operational standby they were still liable to be called on whenever a Maximum Effort was planned. However, as losses began to mount – for example, No 92 Group lost eleven of the 105 aircraft it sent to Duisburg on the night of 31 July – there was increased pressure to remove the OTUs from operations. Again there was no immediate change of policy and the records show heavy losses on other raids in 1942, one of the worst being five out of thirteen Wellingtons from No 16 OTU over Düsseldorf on 10/11 September.

With the entry to service of the trio of 'heavy' bombers, the existing training organisation of the OTUs had to be modified in the light of experience. The comments that had been made when the Wellington was introduced of pilots and crews needing appropriate training for advanced aircraft, was even more relevant for the four-engined types.

The Handley Page Halifax MkI bomber, powered with four Rolls Royce engines.

The twin-engined Avro Manchester. Constant engine problems proved disastrous for the aircraft, although despite its failures, it gave rise to the best RAF bomber of the war: the Lancaster.

HEAVY CONVERSION UNITS

When the Lancaster entered service in early 1942 the initial task of converting crews to the aircraft was undertaken by small Conversion Flights, usually two or three aircraft, within the individual squadrons. This is why you will see in the records reference, for example, to No 106 CU – this being the conversion flight within 106 Squadron. A similar policy had been used for the other heavies. The decision was taken in September 1942 to combine the on-squadron Conversion Flights into special training units as Heavy Conversion Units (HCUs) equipped with Manchesters and Lancasters. Using the Lancaster example, by the end of October the following units had formed:

> No 1654 HCU at Wiglsey (ex 50 and 83 Squadron CFs)
>
> No 1656 HCU at Breighton (ex 103 and 460 Squadrons)
>
> No 1660 HCU at Swinderby (ex 61, 97, 106 and 207 Squadrons)
>
> No 1661 HCU at Skellingthorpe (ex 9, 44 and 49 Squadrons)

Of these, all except No 1656 HCU – which was for No 1 Group – were part of No 5 Group. The initial establishment of sixteen Lancasters and sixteen Manchesters was almost immediately changed to twelve Lancasters plus twenty Manchesters or Halifaxes. With a desire to put as many Lancasters as possible into the operational squadrons even this ratio was soon changed.

The basic HCU course was conducted in a similar format to that of the OTU, albeit over a shorter time frame, and at this point the Flight Engineer was added to the crew. Eventually each of the three operational heavy Groups controlled its own HCUs, with an allocation of three such units per Group – a notional total of fifteen HCUs. By January 1943, with the formation of No 1662 HCU at Blyton, the total number of units had reached eleven, with the plan being to increase this to sixteen by November. This policy of keeping the HCUs under the Groups for which they provided crews, gradually became more unworkable as the front-line expanded and the training organisation grew but it was not until September 1944 that their admin and control was brought together under No 7 (HCU) Group, headquartered at Grantham.

By April 1943 Bomber Command was over 100 crews short of establishment and, as a short-term fix, it was decided to increase the intake of each OTU course from sixteen to eighteen crews every two weeks. The overall output requirement was set at 383 crews a month (from March) rising to 622 crews by December. The number of bomber OTUs peaked in December 1943 with a total of twenty-two and a half units; a strength of around 1,300 aircraft, and thousands of air and ground personnel.

Bill Carmen arrived at Upper Heyford (No 16 OTU) in July 1943:

> 'Here at the OTU the aircrew came together to get to know each other and choose whom they would be happy to fly with, eventually being formed into a crew. The Wellington became our 'chariot' and we realised that from now on we were at the start of a serious business. On one occasion our crew were grouped outside the Control Tower waiting our turn to take over a Wimpey from another crew. It pulled up by the Tower and suddenly its starboard engine burst into flames. The occupying aircrew evacuated at maximum speed out of the front hatch – they were like rabbits coming out of a rabbit hole ahead of a ferret. My crew were by then pelting around to the far side of the Tower out of harms way. The Station fire-engine leapt into action but for some reason couldn't raise any pressure in their hose and the nozzle hung limp at the business end. This situation pro-

Wellington bomber airmen disembark from a truck, ready to fly another mission.

voked some explicit ribald remarks from the aircrews. With bullets flying about in all directions as the ammunitions belts 'cooked' in the heat, the poor old Wimpey, its geodetic skeleton now exposed, sank to its knees. By this time we had all taken cover inside the Control Tower.'

Arthur Harris in his post-war Despatch on War Operations highlighted the problem of finding instructors:

'...It was quickly found that only aircrew with

Fire damage to a Wellington bomber reveals the geodetic structure of the fuselage.

operational experience could successfully train crews from the OTU stage onwards, but owing to the constant expansion of the front line, and the rate of casualties at the height of the war, which did not allow for a large number of tour-expired aircrew becoming available as instructors, there was always a lag in the number of pilot instructors. For a considerable period there was also a deficiency in the number of navigators and air bombers. In consequence of this, until well into 1944, training units had to struggle along with their strength of instructors well below establishment.'

By 1943 a full-size OTU had an establishment of fifty-four aircraft and was capable of producing thirty-two crews a month in summer and twenty-two a month in winter. November brought another request for a slowing down of output as OTU crews were 'clogging up' the training system further down stream at the HCU stage. In general each unit now had seven courses at any one time, five in training, one on leave and one awaiting posting.

Based at Wellesbourne Mountford, No 22 OTU was typical of a bomber training unit in early 1944. Its aircraft strength comprised eighty aircraft, primarily Wellington IIIs and Xs, but with a number of Martinet Is for target towing (gunnery practice). The course size averaged twenty-eight to thirty crews, a total of 654 students, the majority of them Canadian. In a typical summer month, an OTU of standard size would expect to fly around 5,000 hours, just under half of which would be at night.

LANCASTER FINISHING SCHOOLS

With the Lancaster having proved the most effective of the Command's bombers it had been decided, towards the end of 1943, to equip as many operational Groups as possible with the Avro heavy. No 3 Group was earmarked to join No 1 and No 5 Group as Lancaster operators and the only way to provide enough aircraft was to remove them from the HCUs.

The plan was to equip the HCUs within No 3 and No 5 Group with Stirlings and to give the other HCUs Halifaxes. However, it was recognised that crews would need some degree of Lancaster orientation and whilst at first it was believed that this could be done at squadron level, it was eventually decided to form specialist training units to carry out a short orientation course. Three Lancaster Finishing Schools (LFS) were formed, one for each of the Lancaster-equipped operational Groups and numbered appropriately – No 1 LFS at Lindholme/Hemswell, No 3 LFS at Feltwell and No 5 LFS at Syerston, although 1678 and 1679 HCUs also kept Lancaster elements. The initial intention was that each LFS would train thirty-six crews per fortnight; thus the student pilot would have a four-week course, of forty

Bomber crew getting kitted up ready for a mission.

flying hours, at the HCU, followed by two weeks, with ten flying hours, at the LFS. John Gee, having completed a tour on the Halifax, was sent to No 1 LFS in mid-1944:

'As soon as one got into the seat one could feel that there was something different about this aeroplane. All the controls were easily to hand and the Perspex cover over the cockpit was slightly higher than the top of the fuselage, giving the pilot a commanding view. As soon as I took my first flight I could feel the difference, it was wonderfully balanced and light on the controls, it handled more like a fighter than a bomber.'

Bomb Aimer Don Clay was at the same LFS in August:

'The ground work consisted mainly of getting to know our various stations and equipment as well as escape procedures for baling out and dinghy drill. One of our final sorties at the LFS was fighter affiliation and by the end of the exercise our 'lad' left us in no doubt that, given the correct 'gen' by the gunners, no Jerry fighters would ever mark us down as a kill. With our last exercise at LFS we were sent home on leave for a week and told to report back before being posted to an operational squadron.'

As an example of how variable the training requirement was, there were three major changes in 1944. In April the Command was seeking to increase the supply of crews, primarily due to a period of heavier than expected losses. However, by July the War Cabinet was worried about an overall manpower shortage and was looking for

reductions in the training system. The decision was taken to stop expansion of the bomber training organisation and to reverse the trend in order to have fifteen OTUs at the end of the year, further reducing to six by March 1945.

The August 1944 Aircrew Training Bulletin included an article entitled 'Bomber Command Training' and this provides a neat overview of the training system. 'The training organisation is divided into five stages:

1. Operational Training Unit – ten weeks with forty day and forty night hours.

2. Air Crew School – two weeks with no flying.

3. Conversion Unit – four weeks with twenty day and twenty night hours.

4. Lancaster Finishing School – two weeks with five day and five night hours.

5. Squadron conversion – one week with five hours day and five hours night.

The Bulletin went on to address the OTU phase in more detail:

The flying course starts with conversion to the Wellington aircraft, gradually progresses through various stages and ends up with a leaflet raid in a Wellington over enemy-occupied Europe. The syllabus includes the following exercises:

1. Synthetic training. Link trainer, AM Bombing Teacher, clay pigeon shooting, turret training.

2. Gunnery. Combat manoeuvres, air-to-sea firing, air-to-air firing, fighter affiliation exercise day and night.

Lancaster crew during 1943. It was essential for a crew to have confidence in its 'skipper' and to work as a team.

3. Bombing. High-level bombing by day and night, bombing on cross-countries, infra-red bombing, demonstration of pathfinder technique and target indicators.

4. Navigation. DR navigation, cross-countries, radar training.

5. Operational training. Night exercises with night fighters, searchlight and anti-aircraft organisation in this country, leaflet raid over enemy territory.

6. Drills. Dinghy, parachute, fire, oxygen, crash drills.

7. Operational procedures. Darky, searchlight homing, SOS.

The Halifax MkIII which was the most effective of the variants.

June 1944 was the high point of the training machine in terms of aircraft numbers, with a strength of 2,018 aircraft at forty-four units, comprising twenty-two OTUs, fifteen HCUs, three LFSs and four 'miscellaneous training units' such as the Pathfinder Navigation Training Unit (PFNTU). These aircraft were housed at fifty-nine airfields and employed thousands of air and ground personnel.

THE FINAL MONTHS AND RUN DOWN OF STRENGTH

Accident rates at OTUs were always a problem, as evidenced by the fact that over 8,000 Bomber Command aircrew lost their lives in training. Air Vice-Marshal J Gray, AOC No 91 Group, sent the following message to No 22 OTU:

'Congratulations on October's 3,600 flying hours without accident, and this after four months of over 1,000 hours per accident.'

Sadly, the following month had its share of tragedy with two fatal Wellington accidents on 20 November with LN460 exploding in mid-air and MF509 crashing in Wales, both with the loss of their crews.

However, the predicted loss rates, and thus the expansion plans for the training machine, were amended during the latter part of 1944 as losses were generally lower than expected. On 29 September 1944, the War Cabinet had instructed that overall strength was not to exceed eighty-five heavy bomber squadrons by the end of the year and the number of training establishments should be reduced. It was proposed to run an establishment of seventeen OTUs, seventeen HCUs and four LFSs but almost as soon as the ink was dry on a plan it was amended, both in terms of the number and strength of units and the aircraft types allocated to each. The peak was achieved in December with eighty-five heavy bomber squadrons and seventeen Mosquito squadrons; falling loss rates and reduced aircrew wastage in training, and through accidents, brought about a rapid run-down of training units and a re-equipment programme.

Having been taken out of Main Force, the Stirling had been a key part of the HCU operation; but with an increasing number of Lancasters becoming available in the latter part of 1944 it was decided to re-equip each Stirling HCU with an establishment of thirty-two Lancasters and to incorporate within them the role performed by the LFSs. First to undergo this transformation was No 3 Groups' 1651 and 1653 HCUs, although three more Stirling HCUs had acquired

The Avro Lancaster. Powered by four Rolls-Royce Merlin engines and with excellent all-round performance, it became the best strategic bomber of the Second World War.

The Short Stirling heavy bomber. Although the Stirling was the first of the 'heavies' to enter service, build up was slow because of production problems.

Right: The de Havilland Mosquito. A 4,000lb bomb-load and the range to reach Berlin added a new dimension to Bomber Command for diversionary and nuisance raids.

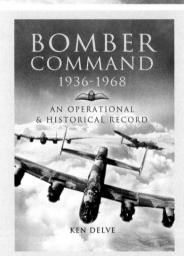

Lancasters by January 1945. A similar re-equipment programme was also instituted for the Halifax-equipped training units.

The Operational Training Units were also undergoing change during this period and by the end of 1944, five OTUs had been disbanded – but four new ones had been created or re-equipped and expanded! This was, however, a short-lived 'expansion' and the overall trend was one of reduction – with spare aircrew looking for employment.

The final operational losses of OTU aircraft occurred on the night of 14/15 January 1945, when three out of a force of 126 aircraft never made it back to their bases (one from 27 OTU at Lichfield and two from 30 OTU at Hixon). The mission was an Operation *Sweepstake*, a diversionary flight over the North Sea that did not penetrate enemy territory but was classed as an operational mission.

By 1945 courses were being cancelled all the way through the training system, from basic pilot training onwards, and trained aircrew were being sent to holding units pending decisions on where they would end up. Many never made it to a squadron. The final fatalities during the wartime period occurred on 20 April 1945 when Wellington LP760, of 19 OTU, took-off from Kinloss at 11.52 and appeared to explode in mid-air; all six on board were killed.

By May 1945 the run-down of operational squadrons had commenced and towards the end of the year Bomber Command was already a shadow of its former self.

DEVELOPING THE PLAN; THE FORMATION OF 617 SQUADRON

While David Maltby and his new crew were getting acquainted at Woodhall Spa, a few miles away – at 5 Group headquarters in Grantham – an audacious plan was being developed. After years of experiments and tests, and months of meetings and lobbying, the assistant chief designer of Vickers-Armstrong Aviation Section, Barnes Wallis, had finally been given permission to go ahead with developing a new weapon to attack the German dams in the Ruhr and Eder valleys.

By Charles Foster

This article was extracted from Charles Foster's book *Breaking The Dams -The Story of Dambuster David Maltby and his Crew* and is reproduced here by permission of Pen and Sword Books Ltd.

The exact timing of what happened during the formation of the new squadron have been the subject of confusion over the years (not least because Gibson himself muddied the water with his account in *Enemy Coast Ahead*, where he elided some events and invented others). Even the two most authoritative accounts, by John Sweetman and Richard Morris, still disagree on some dates, for instance that of the first meeting between Gibson and Cochrane. It may be helpful, therefore, to set out a chronology from Friday 12 March to Wednesday 31 March as David would have seen it, in a narrative put together with the help of Robert Owen, 617 Squadron's official historian.

FRIDAY 12 MARCH

Gibson finished his tour of operations after a flight to Stuttgart, and prepared to leave RAF Coningsby. His own account says that his new job was supposed to be at Group HQ writing a manual for new bomber pilots, but the adjutant at 106 Squadron, probably writing with hindsight, recorded on Sunday 14 March that Gibson had been posted to 'form a new squadron'.

WEDNESDAY 17 MARCH

At the headquarters of Bomber Command in High Wycombe, the Senior Air Staff Officer, Air Vice Marshal R D Oxland, wrote two important memos, which officially started the process of forming a new squadron. First he wrote to the G/C Ops at Bomber Command, Air Cdre S O Bufton, stating that the Commander in Chief [Harris] had decided 'this afternoon' that a new squadron should be formed. On the same day his information was passed to the Air Officer Commanding No.5 Group, Air Vice Marshal the Hon Sir Ralph Cochrane. Oxland also wrote directly to Cochrane describing the new weapon called Upkeep, a spherical bomb which if spun and dropped from a height of 100 ft, at about 200 mph, would travel 1,200 yards.

It is proposed to use this weapon in the first instance against a large dam in Germany, which, if breached, will have serious consequences in the neighbouring industrial area... The operation against this dam will not, it is thought, prove particularly dangerous, but it will undoubtedly require skilled crews. Volunteer crews will, therefore, have to be carefully selected from the squadrons in your Group.

It is worth noting that the weapon is here called a spherical bomb, but after further trials the design was changed to a large cylinder, much the shape and size of

he roller used on a cricket field. This was also the day
n which the 97 Squadron Operations Record book
ecords the return to the Squadron of 'F/L G. H. Maltby
sic] from 1485 S & G Flight [sic]'.

THURSDAY 18 MARCH

*In the afternoon, Gibson was called in to meet
Cochrane, and asked to do 'one last trip.'*
(Morris says that this meeting happened on
Monday 15 March.) In Enemy Coast Ahead,
*Gibson wrote that nothing happened for two
days after that, but in fact it seems that there
was a gap of only one day.* The 97 Squadron
ORB records the transfer of Fort, Hatton,
Nicholson, Stone, Simmonds and Williams from
207 Squadron on this day.

FRIDAY 19 MARCH

*Gibson was called to another meeting with
Cochrane. This time the Station Commander of
RAF Scampton, Air Cdre Charles Whitworth,
was also present. Gibson was asked to form a
special squadron. Gibson says that he then spent
another two days at Grantham in meetings
selecting 'equipment, bodies, erks [groundcrew],
aircrew'. Two of the people he names: the man
with the red moustache called Cartwright, and a
Sqn Ldr May – the others obviously made less of
an impression on him.* He says that it took him
an hour to pick his pilots, and that he wrote the
names down on a piece of paper and handed
them over. 'I had picked them all myself because,
from my own personal knowledge, I believed
them to be the best bomber pilots available. I
knew that each one of them had already done
his full tour of duty and should really now be
having a well-earned rest; and I knew also that
there was nothing any of them would want less
than this rest when they heard that there was an
exciting operation on hand.'*

t is this paragraph that has led to the myth that the
ilots at 617 Squadron were personally selected by
Gibson. He goes on to compound the story with a
escription of finding them all waiting for him, and an
mpromptu party in the officers' mess, on the day he
rrived at Scampton. Paul Brickhill repeats this version
f events in *The Dam Busters* book, and the movie
ollows the same course, with a role for his pint-drinking
log, the famous Nigger.

The truth is that the process was much more drawn
ut, and the crews arrived over a period of about ten
lays. It is probable that only the pilots who were to be
ransferred from 57 Squadron, based at Scampton,
would have been in the mess on the day Gibson arrived,
o he could not have possibly spent the first evening
nocking back pints with the whole lot. We know that
Gibson certainly asked for some pilots by name, because
e spoke to Mick Martin, Joe McCarthy and David

Shannon, and maybe some others, by phone. Why did he
choose to over-elaborate the story? The answer, as
Richard Morris has discovered, is because Gibson's
name appeared on an article, written by a Ghost writer,
in the *Sunday Express* later in 1943, where the writer –
presumably an Air Ministry public relations officer –
credited Gibson with the selection, not only of all the
pilots, but of the entire squadron. Choosing twenty or so
pilots might just have been feasible, but finding another
120 aircrew was most unlikely. In fact, Gibson didn't
even know all of his own crew before 617 Squadron, and
treated some of its members with an arrogance
bordering on contempt. However when the *Sunday
Express* article was incorporated wholesale into the draft
of *Enemy Coast Ahead*, Gibson never bothered to
change it.

SUNDAY 21 MARCH

Although Gibson says that he had spent two days at
Grantham on administrative duties, once again it must
have been not much more than one, since he definitely
arrived at Scampton on the Sunday afternoon. No pilots
or other aircrew were waiting for him, but it seems that
some of the administrative staff must have been ready to
start work the next morning. Two NCOs, Flt Sgt G E
Powell and Sgt Jim Heveron came from 57 Squadron
and were obviously deemed suitable. The Adjutant,
however, wasn't and Gibson got rid of him, asking for an
old colleague from 106 Squadron, Flt Lt Harry
Humphries.

Scampton's yellowy-red brick buildings still look
much as they did during the war, except that most of the
old flat roofs have been replaced. There is only one
flying unit based at the station now – the famous Red
Arrows display team – which means that many buildings
are unused, but they retain the feel of a pre-war life style.
Peering through the windows of the Officers' Mess you
can imagine the leather armchairs, the wind-up
gramophone, the waiter with the tray of drinks. Here is
the rugby pitch, over there the squash courts, there the
base of the old cricket pavilion. The four C type hangars
form an arc on the south-east side of the airfield, and
attached to each is a small two storey administration
block. The block attached to No.2 Hangar is the one
which housed the 617 Squadron offices, with the
squadron commander occupying the top right corner,
and the adjutant next to him. One day in June 1943, two
months after Operation *Chastise*, Gibson and Maltby sat
in that office, trying to look busy while an Air Ministry
photographer shot a series of expensive colour
transparencies for publicity purposes.

At the time of *Chastise*, Scampton still had grass
runways. The airfield sits atop a slight escarpment with
excellent natural drainage, so the runway area did not
often get boggy enough to jeopardise the flying of heavy
aircraft. From aerial pictures taken at the time (which
can be seen in the small museum in Hangar No 1) you
can see the hedgerows which were painted on the grass
to fool any passing German bomber.

The bouncing bomb mastermind, Barnes Wallis.

I distinctly remember discussing with my crew the question of whether we should volunteer or not, and I seem to think that Joe McCarthy did likewise on the same day. I was not aware of how or when David reached his decision. Can't remember how I was advised that our transfer to Scampton was official, but it was certainly not by Gibson.

He is also fairly sure that they all transferred the few miles to Scampton in a crew bus, and has the distinct memory of a gathering in the ante-room of the Officers' Mess in the evening. Perhaps this was the evening that Gibson wrote about in *Enemy Coast Ahead*, although some of the pilots, such as Mick Martin, were still not at Scampton by this Thursday. (Martin arrived on Wednesday 31 March.)

WEDNESDAY 24 MARCH

Humphries arrived at Scampton. The new squadron (still unnumbered) was described as being 'formed on ordinary Lancasters'. Some aircrew were ordered to report on this day, but it is not clear whether any actually did. Anyway, Gibson was not there to greet them. He had travelled by train and car down to Weybridge in Surrey for his first meeting with Barnes Wallis. To Wallis' embarrassment, he soon realised that he did not have the authority to divulge the target to Gibson.

THURSDAY 25 MARCH

The squadron now had a number, 617, and was reported 'ready to fly'. Nine pilots are listed as being transferred to the new squadron on that day, including the three who came from 97 Squadron: Flt Lts Les Munro, a New Zealander, Joe McCarthy, an American serving in the RCAF, and David Maltby. Their transfer and that of their crews, are all listed in the 97 Squadron Operations Record Book on that day. (The other six pilots transferred on 25 March would seem to have been Flt Lt David Shannon, from 8 Group, Sqn Ldr Henry Maudslay and PO Les Knight from 50 Squadron, FO Norman Barlow from 61 Squadron and Sgts Cyril Anderson and Bill Townsend from 49 Squadron.)

Les Munro and Joe McCarthy were both coming towards the end of their first tours. David was starting his second. In recent correspondence with me Les wrote:

> 'To Wallis'
> embarrassment,
> he soon realised
> that he did not
> have the authority
> to divulge the
> target to Gibson.'

Joe McCarthy

SATURDAY 27 MARCH

Gibson at least began to get a better idea of what was expected from the squadron when a set of 'most secret' orders was given to him by Gp Capt HV Satterly, Senior Air Staff Officer at 5 Group. Without being told the exact targets, Gibson was informed that the squadron would be attacking a number of lightly defended targets in moonlight with a final approach at 100ft at a precise speed of about 240mph. The orders stated that, in preparation for the attack, it would be 'convenient to practice this over water' and crews should be able to release their 'mine' within forty yards of a specified release point. Night flying would be simulated by making the pilot and bomb aimer wear special amber coloured goggles and fitting blue Perspex screens to the windows.

By now, a number of ordinary Lancasters had arrived for training purposes and in the afternoon, the first crew got airborne. Flt Lt Bill Astell was despatched to photograph nine lakes that Satterly had identified as being suitable for practice.

SUNDAY 28 MARCH

Gibson decided to try out low flying over water himself. With Hopgood and Young on board, he went off to Derwent Reservoir in Derbyshire. In daylight the flying was not too difficult, but when dusk fell it became a lot harder, and they narrowly avoided an accident.

MONDAY 29 MARCH

Gibson was summoned to Group HQ and told the target by Cochrane. He was shown models of the Möhne

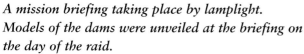

Derwent Reservoir in Derbyshire – one of the dams used to practice low level cross-country flying.

A mission briefing taking place by lamplight. Models of the dams were unveiled at the briefing on the day of the raid.

and Sorpe dams – the model of the Möhne, dramatically unveiled to all the crews at the briefing on the day of the raid, can still be seen in the Imperial War Museum.

WEDNESDAY 31 MARCH

Training was gathering pace by this stage, and David and his crew made their first training flight on this day. The Avro factories were still adapting the special Lancasters that 617 Squadron would need for the raid,

so for much of April these flights took place on ordinary aircraft. David flew for two hours on what was described as a 'low level cross-country and bombing' exercise.

During the next six weeks, David and his crew would fly on another twenty-three training flights, mainly low-level cross country and bombing. Various routes had been devised and the reservoirs at Derwent Reservoir in Derbyshire, Eyebrook near Uppingham and Abberton near Colchester were used for runs at low level over water. *The Dam Busters* film has a scene where a farmer writes a letter of complaint to the Air Ministry about the effect on his egg production. This was based on the

An example of an Avro factory production line. Lancaster cockpits and front nose gun turrets, awaiting assembly.

A female worker making adjustments on a Lancaster in the Avro assembly line.

truth, as a number of complaints from farmers were received during this period. It's not surprising, the noise generated by flying at the astonishing low level at which they were practising must have been devastating – many church spires are well over 200ft in height, and the tower of Lincoln Cathedral is 271ft.

The impression is sometimes given that the crews spent all their time in these six weeks practising, but in fact David and his crew were only airborne on average every other day for a total of some 29 hours. Only three aircraft were equipped with the special tinted cockpit windows which allowed the simulation of night flying, so crews had to take turns, and use other aircraft for other types of training. There were several gaps of two or three days, and one of five days, between flights.

J FOR JOHNNY; MALTBY'S CREW

On Wednesday 17 March 1943, David Maltby reported back to 97 Squadron at the familiar RAF Woodhall Spa to start his second tour. The next day, bomb aimer John Fort, flight engineer William Hatton, navigator Vivian Nicholson, wireless operator Antony Stone and air gunners Harold Simmonds and Austin Williams all arrived, after just a month in 207 Squadron at RAF Langar. This was a complete crew except for, of course, a pilot. These six men had all come together in a Lancaster conversion unit at RAF Swinderby at the beginning of the year, but they arrived there by a variety of routes.

VIVIAN NICHOLSON

By common consent the navigator was the next most skilled person in a heavy bomber crew after the pilot. In David Maltby's team, this role was performed by its youngest member, a smiling lad with crinkly hair from

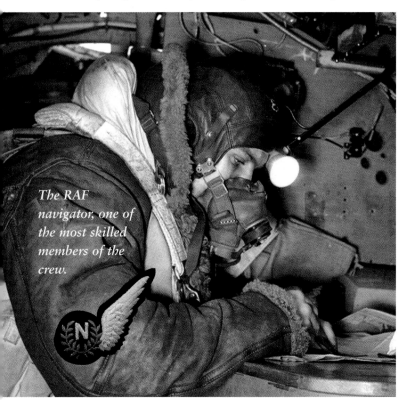

The RAF navigator, one of the most skilled members of the crew.

Co Durham named Vivian Nicholson. The Nicholson family came from Sherburn, once one of the dozens of pit communities that ring the city of Durham – now a commuter village. Before nationalisation, the local mines were owned by the Lambton family, and the pub at the village crossroads still bears their name. (The sometime head of the family, Viscount Lambton, had his moment in the national limelight when he had to resign from the Heath government in the 1970s after his affair with a prostitute was exposed. The press photos of the time show him in a pair of particularly sinister dark glasses, which added to his somewhat seedy reputation.) The collieries closed in the 1950s, but at the time the Nicholson family were growing up most local people were employed at the collieries.

'Vivian was the eldest of eight children, all boys. I sat in his brother Cyril's house on a summer morning as he went through the names: Vivian, Arthur, Cyril, Everett, Ian, Ivan, Raymond and Francis. Two died young: Ian at the age of 8, and Ivan in infancy. Two more now live in the USA. Cyril, Raymond and Francis still live locally, Cyril in the same street in which he was brought up, in a house his parents also once owned. Vivian's parents – Arthur and Elizabeth – and their boys were a respectable church-going family and their paternal grandfather, Harle Nicholson, was the local churchwarden. The family album still shows a photo with three of the boys in identical smart Sunday suits. Arthur Nicholson had a joinery and undertaking business, and also owned some of the houses in the village. When he left the local school, Vivian was apprenticed in the family business but then, even before he turned 18, he volunteered to join the RAF.'

After initial training in No 1 Initial Training Wing in Babbacombe, near Torquay, Vivian was packed off to Canada on the British Commonwealth Air Training Plan. Canada, with its wide open spaces and distance from the main theatres of conflict in Europe, was ideal for aircrew training, and over 150,000 people from Britain, the Commonwealth countries and the USA, were sent there during the war. He started his training in Canada but then went on to Tuscaloosa, Alabama in the USA for part of his course. Even though the USA was not yet in the war, it was already providing training facilities for the Allies.

In December 1941, round about the time the Japanese attacked Pearl Harbor and brought the USA into the war, he sent his parents a picture of himself and 'a lad from Sheffield' called Mick Smith.

'We have been pals, with Harry Sherwood, (and Doc Webb from Willington if he had been with us, poor lad) right through our course from London to Tuscaloosa.' He added: *'All the best from U.S.A. A merry Xmas.'*

Besides the training in navigation itself, there were a number of other courses the aspiring navigators needed to pass, such as map reading, armaments, Morse Code, instrument and radio direction-finding, reconnaissance and aerial photography. Navigation itself required a lot of mathematical skill. No calculators or other mechanical help existed then, although there were complicated slide rules which helped with some of the calculations. A navigator had to learn how to find the position of his aircraft using 'dead reckoning'. By knowing the direction, speed and course on which you were travelling you were able to work out your 'air position'. You then compared this with your 'ground position' by recording the time you reached various known places on your map. You could therefore calculate the variation caused by the wind – the 'drift' – and tell the pilot which course to set. That was the theory, at least, but of course in practice it was much more difficult.

By the late summer of 1942 Vivian's specialist navigator training was at an end, and the work of getting him ready to fly in a bomber crew began. He was sent to No 10 OTU at RAF St Eval, Cornwall, in September 1942. He arrived there at the same time as bomb aimer John Fort and wireless operator Antony Stone, and it is likely that the trio teamed up there. Some of the training flights in this Unit took place on anti-submarine patrols in Whitley aircraft, but it doesn't seem that Vivian took part in these. All three arrived at No 1660 Conversion Unit at RAF Swinderby in January 1943, at the same time as William Hatton and Harold Simmonds, and probably crewed up there. A month or so later, they were ready for operations and they all left for 207 Squadron at RAF Langar in Nottinghamshire.

ANTONY STONE

Winchester's sometime town crier, Alan Kinge, has done a lot to keep the story of Antony Stone and his family in the forefront of local people's minds by writing articles in the local press and organising an exhibition in the city library. I was lucky enough to track down Alan with the help of the library, and he passed on to me what he knew about the family history, and contact details for the family.

Antony Joseph Bazeley Stone was the younger son of a family of two boys. His older brother Edgar is still alive but was not well enough to talk to me when I contacted the family early in 2007. Edgar's son Michael, however, was happy to help. Born a few years after the war, like me, Michael remembers hearing a lot about his uncle when he was growing up, but of course, never met him.

Edgar and Antony's father, Joseph Stone, had an eventful life. He was Jewish, and had been born in Russia at the end of the nineteenth century. The family legend is that he was brought to London by the Rothschild family, who were certainly involved in helping Jewish families escape the pogroms of the time. He trained as a barber in Hackney and joined the Rifle

Brigade at the beginning of the First World War. This brought him to Winchester, and he stayed there after the war where he met and married a Hampshire girl called Dorothy Grace Bazeley. Joe set up as a barber in a shop in Jewry Street in the city. Their second son was born at home in Nuns Road, Winchester on 5 December 1920.

Antony went first to the local Hyde School and sang in the choir at St Bartholomew's Church. A picture of the choir still exists and a school friend, Alan House, recalls that no fewer than four other boys, of the seven sitting in the same row as Antony, were later to join the RAF. Antony then went to Peter Symonds School in Winchester. He decided to train as a chef, and went up to London to do so, studying at the Westminster Technical Institute. He worked at various well known restaurants, including Quaglino's, the Dorchester and the Ritz; cooking at one time, Michael recalls being told, for the King and Queen.

In 1940 he volunteered for the RAF, and was called up, in November 1940, to the same Reception Centre at Uxbridge as David had been through a few months earlier. He was selected for wireless operator training, and passed through various training centres at Thorney Island, Yatesbury and Bassingbourn.

Training as a wireless operator not only involved the obvious: sending and receiving of signals and learning Morse Code. By the end of the course, operators had to be able to read and transmit Morse Code at a speed of at least eighteen words a minute. There were also a large number of 'Q codes' which had to be memorised. These were three letter codes, all beginning with 'Q', that were requests or instructions to be sent to and from the base, covering such things as requests from the base for weather updates (QBZ) or from the aircraft for permission to land (QFO). Wireless training also meant gaining a lot of theoretical and practical knowledge about radios and all the other electrical equipment on board. This meant that the wireless operator on a heavy bomber often picked up other ancillary duties. On Operation *Chastise*, for instance, it became his job to start and supervise the rotation mechanism for the special mine ten minutes before the bombing run began.

At the time Antony was passing through the system, wireless operators also had to have gunnery training, although this requirement was removed later in the war. His last piece of specialist training was therefore at No 1 Air Gunnery School, at RAF Pembrey in Carmarthenshire. Then it was on to No 10 OTU at St Eval, where his path crossed with Vivian Nicholson and John Fort.

By the time he arrived at 617 Squadron Antony was engaged to a nurse at the Royal Hampshire County Hospital, Peggy Henstridge, although it's not certain when the relationship began.

JOHN FORT

John Fort was born on the Lancashire side of the

'A navigator had to learn how to find the position of his aircraft using 'dead reckoning'.

Pennines, in the cotton town of Colne, on 14 January 1912. He was one of six brothers. After attending Christchurch School in the town, he went into the RAF in 1929 to train as an apprentice, going to the No. 1 School of Technical Training at RAF Halton in Buckinghamshire. This was the famous training establishment set up by Lord Trenchard ('the father of the RAF') to supply the technicians needed to support aircrew and maintain aircraft. After completing the three year course he was posted to the Central Flying School and then went to sea in the aircraft carrier HMS *Glorious*. (Between 1918 and 1937 the RAF operated the aircraft which flew on aircraft carriers, and supplied its own ground staff to service them.)

Back on dry land, he continued in groundcrew until the second year of the war, when he volunteered for aircrew training. Selected as a specialist bomb aimer (or air bomber, to give the job its proper name) he went off to a Bombing and Gunnery School, where students were taught a lot of theory as well as practical aspects such as map reading and simulator training, learning exactly where to drop the weapon. They moved on to practice air-to-ground bombing runs over ranges where they dropped 25 lb smoke bombs.

This is where they developed the real skills. The bomb aimer took over the navigation of the aircraft from the navigator as they approached the target and began a bombing run. It was he who would call out to the pilot over the intercom the small direction changes needed, from his position lying flat out in the nose. From a height of 1,000 ft, the bomb aimer would be expected to be able to hit a target with an accuracy of under 50 yards.

At the end of his course John had done well enough to be offered a commission and so it was as a Pilot Officer he arrived at No 10 OTU in September 1942, at RAF St Eval. After completing the course there, he met Vivian Nicholson and Antony Stone, and went with them to 1660 Conversion Unit, and on to 207 Squadron. The citation for the DFC, that he later received for Operation *Chastise*, says that he had completed one operation before joining 617 Squadron. As there appears to be no record of him flying on an operation in 207 Squadron, he may have been credited with one while at the OTU, as some anti-submarine patrols were flown from there.

HAROLD SIMMONDS

Harold Thomas Simmonds was born on Christmas Day 1921, the only son of Thomas and Elizabeth Simmonds. Their only daughter, Grace, was some five years younger. His parents were both from Burgess Hill in East Sussex, and they settled in the town after they had married. They had met while they were both working in service, Thomas as a gardener.

Burgess Hill has expanded hugely since the 1920s, and is now firmly within the London commuter area, but when Harold and Grace were growing up, it only had a population of a few thousand. However, ninety men from the town and the surrounding area were killed during the Second World War, and are commemorated in the publication *The Men of Burgess Hill*, compiled by Guy Voice. Would that every town in Britain had a similar publication – research like mine would have been made a lot easier!

Harold went to London Road School and later worked in local government. Soon after the war started, Harold volunteered for the RAF. He started his service in groundcrew, serving at Kemble in Gloucestershire and Mount Batten near Plymouth. However, he had always wanted to fly, and eventually he was selected for aircrew training, going to the No 2 Air Gunners School in Dalcross, near Inverness.

At some point in 1942 he started going out with a girl called Phyllis, although his sister Grace doesn't know her surname, or where they met. She does have a photograph of the pair together, which was captioned as being taken in Warrington, Cheshire, in 1942.

The training for gunnery took less time than any of the other specialist jobs in a Lancaster, but the trainees still had to spend up to thirteen weeks firing guns on the ground and later at drogues towed by aircraft. They also had to learn how to fix faults, strip their guns down and maintain them – essential skills if they were to keep them working while up in the air. Sometimes they were blindfolded when practicing these skills, just to make the conditions more difficult.

The training system meant that gunners and flight engineers only joined up with navigators, bomb aimers and wireless operators at the final stage of the process, in the Conversion Unit. Thus it was that Harold Simmonds first met Vivian Nicholson, John Fort and Antony Stone at 1660 Conversion Unit at Swinderby, where they were all posted there on 5 January 1943.

WILLIAM HATTON

The last of the five who crewed up with David Maltby at 97 Squadron, and were to fly on the Dams Raid two months later, was flight engineer William Hatton. Born in Wakefield on 24 March 1920, he was one of four children: two boys and two girls. He went to Holy Trinity and Thornes House School in the town.

Like Harold Simmonds – with whom he became friendly enough to give a photo which was left behind in his personal effects – when Bill first joined the RAF he was placed in groundcrew, training at both No 10 and No 2 Schools of Technical Training. In May 1941, he went to RAF Speke in Liverpool and worked servicing aircraft in the Merchant Ship Fighter Unit. This was a short lived scheme whereby Hawker Hurricanes were sent to sea on special merchant ships, which were equipped with catapults for launching them. The plan was to enable the Hurricanes to be launched far out at sea to help protect the Atlantic convoys. The only drawback was that they had no way of landing, so the pilot had to bale out of the Hurricane and let the aircraft fall into the sea. As Hatton's spell there drew to a close, the opportunity arose for experienced groundcrew to become flight engineers on heavy bombers. Bill applied and was sent to the only flight engineer training facility, No.4 School of Technical Training at RAF St Athan.

The job of the flight engineer was to look after some of the controls (such as fuel consumption) that were previously the responsibility of a qualified pilot. They were also expected to cope with any mechanical problems which arose whilst airborne. Most flight engineers were also given some rudimentary flying training, so that they could keep the aircraft on a level course if the pilot needed a short break, or in an emergency. After qualifying as a flight engineer, Bill went on to Swinderby, to join 1660 Conversion Unit, where he was to join up with the four others listed.

Not much more than a week before the raid was due to take place (although David would not have yet been aware of exactly when it was likely to be) a decision was taken to replace Sgt Austin Williams as front gunner. There appears to have been some sort of disciplinary reason for this, as Williams was posted to the Air Crew Refresher Course in Brighton. With no other gunners available at Scampton, the net was cast further. No 9 Squadron had just moved from RAF Waddington to RAF Bardney to enable concrete runways to be built at Waddington and amongst its personnel was a spare gunner, Sgt Victor Hill. He was hastily moved the 15 or so miles to Scampton, where he is recorded as arriving on Friday 7 May. When Austin Williams came back to Scampton at the end of May, he was assigned to the crew of Plt Off Bill Divall, who hadn't flown on the raid because of crew sickness. (Divall's was one of the two crews which pulled out at the last minute, a decision which made the final selection easier as there were only nineteen serviceable aircraft, and nineteen crews able to fly.) He stayed with Divall in 617 Squadron for the next five months, and died just 24 hours after his erstwhile crewmates when Divall was shot down over the Dortmund Ems canal on 16 September 1943.

VICTOR HILL

Unlike the rest of David Maltby's crew, Victor Hill had plenty of operational experience. He had flown twenty-two operations on Lancasters between October 1942 and March 1943, and had taken part in some of the war's most famous raids, including the daylight raid on the Schneider works at Le Creusot in France.

Victor Hill had been born in Gloucestershire in 1921. He was an only child, the son of Harry and Catherine Hill, who both worked at Berkeley Castle. He was brought up on the castle estate and went to the local school. After leaving school, he also worked at the castle, as a gardener, where he met a girl called Evelyn Hourihane, whom he married in 1941 at about the time he joined the RAF. Evelyn came from the Rhondda in South Wales, and she moved back to Wales to be near her parents while Vic was away in the RAF, soon after their daughter Valerie was born.

We know that Nicholson, Stone, Fort, Simmonds, Hatton and Williams all joined 207 Squadron on 17 February 1943 and stayed there for less than a month. Three pilots also joined 207 Squadron from 1660 Conversion Unit on the same day, but none of them seem to have been attached to this crew. The 207 Squadron

records are confusing, and it is therefore not clear what they did in this time. They would probably have been treated as 'spares' for a while, which is why William Hatton flew on two operations on 26 and 27 February, with two different pilots. There are entries in the 207 Squadron Operations Record Book during March for a Sgt V Nicholson, a Sgt I H Nicholson, a Sgt J Simmons and a Sgt H T Simmonds, sometimes flying with the same pilot, sometimes with different ones. Entries for both versions of these names are still appearing at the end of March 1943, by which time we know that Vivian Nicholson and Harold Simmonds were both training at 617 Squadron, so there is obviously some sort of error in the records.

What is clear is that the 207 Squadron ORB states that they were all posted out to 97 Squadron on 15 March. It seems likely that because there was no spare pilot for them to work with as a crew, it was therefore decided to send them on to another squadron which had a pilot available. They are recorded in the 97 Squadron ORB as arriving at Woodhall Spa on 18 March.

They were teamed up with David, and spent several days in routine training flights and getting used to each other. Ten days after they all arrived at Woodhall, they were moved together as a crew to the new squadron at Scampton. (On 7 May, Sgt Victor Hill was posted from 9 Squadron to replace Austin Williams as front gunner, thereby completing the crew that would fly on the Dams Raid, and be killed on operations four months later.)

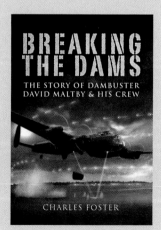

MODIFICATION OF THE LANCASTER BOMBER

A specially modified version of the Lancaster was produced for Operation *Chastise*. It was given the rather unwieldy designation of 'Type 464 Provisioning'.

By Arthur G Thorning

This article was extracted from Arthur G Thorning's *The Dambuster Who Cracked The Dam - The Story of Melvin 'Dinghy' Young* and is reproduced here by permission of Pen and Sword Books Ltd.

The most obvious alteration from the standard Lancaster design was that the bomb doors had been removed and two V-shaped callipers attached to the underside of the fuselage. This structure had bearings by which the cylindrical Upkeep weapon was held, permitting rotation about its axis. The callipers were held firmly against the weapon by cables which could be released by a slip mechanism operated by the bomb aimer. Strong springs would push the callipers away, allowing the weapon to fall clear of the aircraft. On one side there was also a V-belt drive system, powered by a hydraulic motor inside the aircraft, which enabled the weapon to be spun up to the required 500 revolutions per minute (rpm) some minutes before the attack.

A photograph showing the profile of a modified Avro Lancaster. The bomb doors were removed to make way for V-shaped callipers which spun the huge barrel-shaped bomb.

The Upkeep weapon was a cylinder 50 inches in diameter and just under 60 inches long (any longer would not have fitted in the aircraft). It weighed 9,250lbs (4.1 tons), of which 6,600lbs (3 tons) were high explosive. Upkeep was essentially a back-spun depth charge, and was described as such by the Germans when they examined one, although for security reasons the British called it a mine. In order to delay detonation until it had sunk to thirty feet below the water surface, it was equipped with three Admiralty type hydrostatic pistols; detonation devices which could be set to explode the charge at a preset depth. There was also a delayed action fuse which would operate ninety seconds after departure from the aircraft, to minimise the chance of an Upkeep being captured intact although, in the event, one unexploded weapon was found by the Germans.

The hydrodynamics of Upkeep have not been fully analysed even to this day, but the principle behind the backward spin was effectively: to shallow the angle of skip on contact with the water; produce a small amount of lift through the air and, very importantly, keep the weapon in contact with the water face of the dam as it sank. It was also very important that the aircraft wings were level and

Right, above & below: Avro were tasked with reinforcing the fuselage of the Lancaster and fitting it with a frame mechanism to hold the bomb in place. The bomb was too large to house within the aircraft itself so it was designed to hang underneath the airframe in order to accommodate the Ford V8 engine, which was used to spin the bomb up to speed.

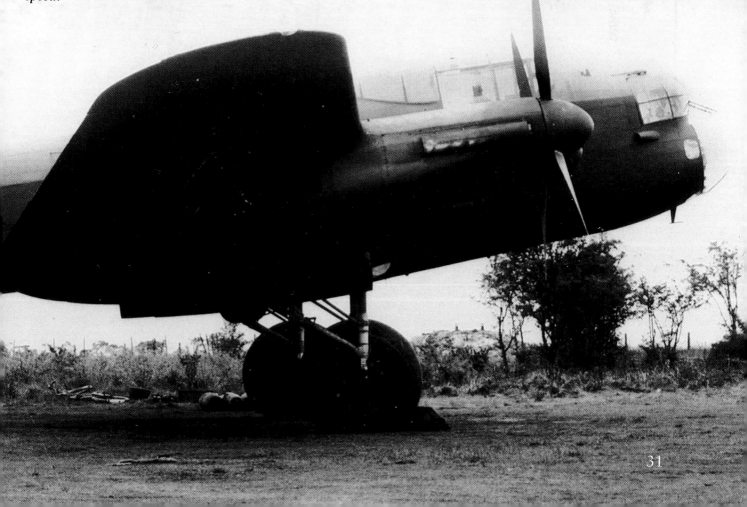

A sequence of photographs highlighting the problems of the bomb release. The first bounce of the bomb created a plume of water so high that it could cause damage to the aircraft.

THE DAMBUSTING BOMB

The bomb was manufactured by Vickers-Armstrong, who employed Barnes Wallis. Orders were placed for 120 Upkeeps, 60 inert casings filled with concrete for practice and the remaining 60 filled with a new explosive, Torpex. This was a scarce material with a compound explosive of 42% RDX, 40% TNT and 18% Aluminium powder. Torpex was the most powerful military explosive available at that time and was poured warm into the mine casings before setting.

60 inches

50 inches

Weight: 9,250lbs (4.1 tons)
Charge weight: 6,600lbs (3 tons)

with no roll motion on release – no easy task – otherwise the cylinder would touch the water on one edge and veer off line. This seems to have happened with one weapon at the Möhne. On each skip, the contact with the water involved the exchange of much energy, especially the first bounce when a large plume of spray would rise dangerously close to the aircraft. In order to reach the dam from the release point 425 to 475 yards away, some three or four bounces could be expected.

In order to save weight and drag, the Lancaster's mid-upper gun turret was removed. This freed the second gunner to operate the nose turret which was more likely to be useful for this raid. Another essential modification was the fitting of two spotlights, one near the nose and one at the rear of the now exposed bomb bay, which were configured to produce two circles of light on the surface below the aircraft. When these circles were touching, forming a figure of eight, the aircraft was at the prescribed height, which was reduced during experiments to a very low figure of 60 feet. The pressure altimeter in the aircraft, although a guide to the pilot, was not accurate enough for this task. The job of observing the circles of light and giving the pilot 'up, down or steady' instructions fell to the navigator during the attack; he observed the circles from the cockpit perspex blister which gave a view downwards.

The combination of removing the streamlining of the bomb doors and hanging a large cylindrical object under the aircraft, protruding into the airflow, had a marked effect on the drag of the aircraft. Trials were carried out at the Aeroplane and Armament Experimental Establishment (A&AEE) at Boscombe Down with an Upkeep 'weapon on' at a weight representative of the fuel state during the attack (60,000lbs) and 'weapon off' returning (42,500lbs). The maximum speed at 11,100 feet, 'weapon on', was 233 mph with a power setting of 3,000 rpm at +9lb/sq in boost (the most available without 'going through the gate' for emergency power) –

converted to 700 feet, the altitude of the Möhne Lake, this equates to a true airspeed of 199 mph in the denser air at this altitude (other factors, for example, propeller efficiency, being assumed unchanged). This probably explains why the crews had to practice diving to achieve the required 220 mph for the attack. With a cruise power setting (2650 rpm, +4 lb/sq in boost) the loaded aircraft achieved 206 mph at 13,600 feet, equivalent to 167 mph at sea level. The operational order for the raid specified 180 mph as the transit speed to the dams but it took the section of three aircraft, led by Melvin, two hours and twenty-six minutes to reach the Möhne – a distance of 425 statute miles, at an average speed of 170mph. Whatever the speed achieved, the flight engineers will have been adjusting the engine controls and monitoring the fuel state very carefully.

The equivalent 'weapon off' cruise speed at the lighter weight (42,500lb) was 238mph measured at 14,000 feet, which equates to 192mph at sea level. Thus the return journey could be flown at higher speed, probably with less concern about fuel consumption and more concern about the approaching dawn. The log of Sergeant Nicholson, David Maltby's navigator, shows a true airspeed of 205mph for most of the return flight. At full power (3,000 rpm and +9 lb/sq in boost) the returning aircraft could achieve 214mph at sea level (256mph measured by A&AEE at 11,600 feet), and may well have flown faster in a dive when crossing the danger area over the Dutch coast.

From the above figures it can be seen that the performance of the Type 464 Lancaster was marginal for the task allotted to it.

The take-off weight was limited to 63,000lbs, so it was necessary to calculate the fuel load carefully. Apparently this job fell to Melvin, though sensibly he took technical advice from the squadron engineers: the fuel carried was 1,750 gallons, enough for roughly seven hours flying.

The re-defined shape of the Avro Lancaster, showing the absence of the mid-upper gun turret and newly adapted bomb bay.

ILLUSTRATION BY JON WILKINSON

AVRO LANCASTER

Length: 69ft 6in

Wingspan: 102ft

Bomb load: up to 22,000lbs

Defensive armament: 8 x .303 Browning machine-guns

Range: 2,530 miles (varied with bomb load)

Engines: 4 x Merlin engines - 1,280 horse power each

Later Packard Merlins: 1,640 horse power each

Speed: 275mph

Crew: 7 (Pilot • Flight Engineer • Nose Gunner • Bomb Aimer • Navigator • Wireless Operator • Rear Gunner)

Performance: max speed at 12,000 ft - 287mph

Surface ceiling: 24,500 ft

Range: with 14,000lb bomb load 1,606 miles

Total Lancaster production: 7366

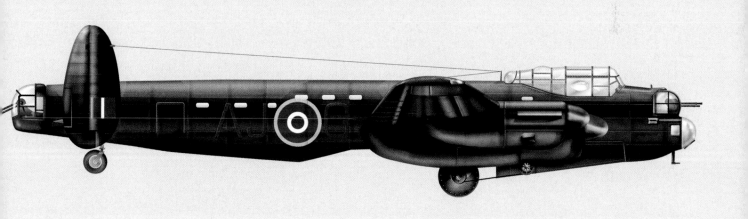

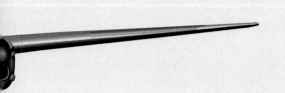

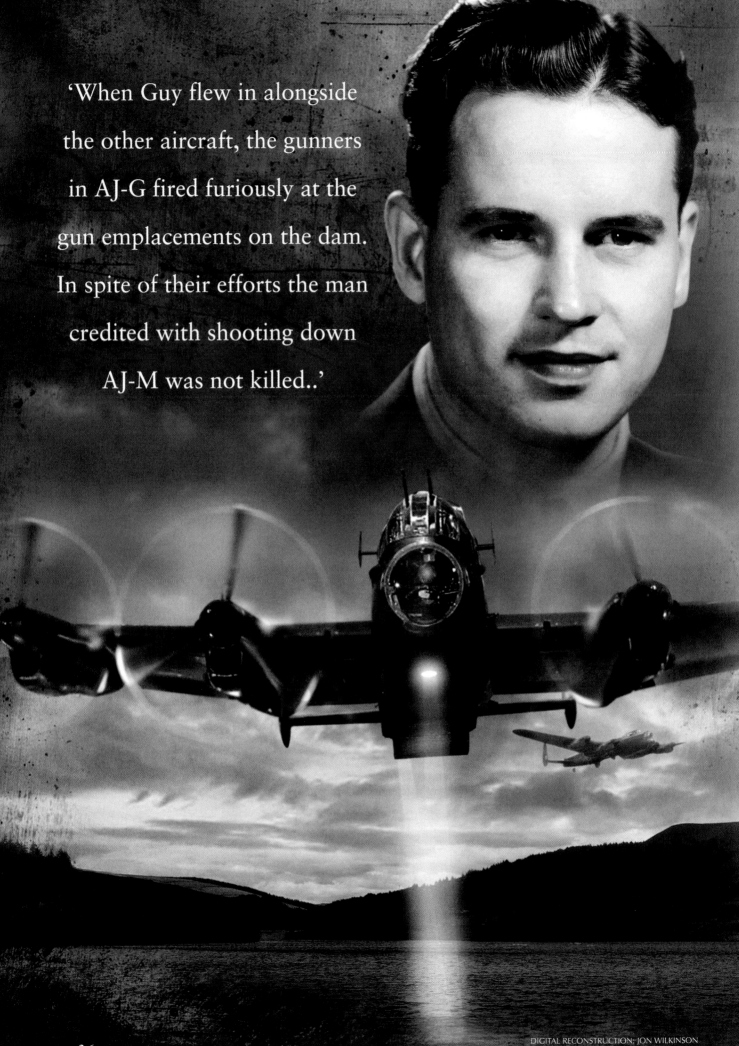

'When Guy flew in alongside the other aircraft, the gunners in AJ-G fired furiously at the gun emplacements on the dam. In spite of their efforts the man credited with shooting down AJ-M was not killed..'

DAMBUSTER GUY GIBSON VC: THE MAN BEHIND THE MISSION

When Guy's leave was cancelled he was dismayed to discover that he had been posted to HQ No 5 Group. He had been hoping that he would be given duties linked with operations during thus time as he was to be rested from operational flying. It now seemed that this would be unlikely.

By Susan Ottaway

This article was extracted from *Dambuster - A Life of Guy Gibson VC* and is reproduced here by permission of Pen and Sword Books Ltd.

This dismay was, however, short-lived as he was soon summoned to the office of Air Vice-Marshal the Hon Ralph Cochrane, AOC No 5 Group, who asked him if he would be prepared to do one more trip. He, of course, agreed but soon began to wonder if he hadn't been a little hasty in his agreement. Although he was not told what the target would be, he began working things out in his own mind from the scant information available and decided that he had probably just volunteered to attack the *Tirpitz*, a task not relished by anyone.

Guy was surprised to learn that he would not take command of an existing squadron but would be instrumental in forming a new one, specifically for the purpose of carrying out this one raid. This was more like it; more than even he had dared to hope. At least it showed that his hard work and excellent results with 106 Squadron had been noticed.

He was told that he would have complete control over the formation of the squadron and that he had the authority to request anything or anyone that he needed. Of the actual raid he was told nothing, only that he would need crews able to fly at low level over water. His first task was to draw up a list of men who he thought would be suitable. The selection of the pilots was relatively easy and most were men known personally to Guy. Some were picked for their expertise and daring; others for their consistency and reliability. Guy had, at this stage in his career, become quite adept at picking the right man for the right job. He was single-minded enough about his own career to recognize the same quality in others and he knew he would need men who would give their all to the task, whatever it might prove to be. With the selection of the other crew members Guy was given some help. Although most had a lot of experience this was not true of all the crews and some were not even close to completing their first tour. The squadron was to be based at RAF Scampton,

which had been home to Guy during his days with 83 Squadron, and was under the command of Group Captain J Whiteworth. The new squadron, which initially was known as Squadron X, was to share the station with 57 Squadron. At the end of March Squadron X was given its proper designation and 617 Squadron was born.

Guy Gibson standing in the cockpit of a Handley Page Hampden. JANET DE GAYNESFORD

The aircraft which would be used for this special task were Avro Lancasters which had to be quite extensively adapted to accommodate the bomb, which had been designed specifically for the raid.

As the crews began arriving at Scampton they found that conditions were somewhat primitive. 49 Squadron, who had previously been at Scampton, had moved out because the airfield was about to be equipped with concrete runways and they had taken almost everything with them. There were no chairs or tables and not enough beds for the hundreds of men that make up a squadron. At first everything had to be scrounged or borrowed and the men themselves made a game of spotting and 'requisitioning' necessary items. The other squadron on the station had to look out for its own equipment. Left alone for even a few minutes it might easily disappear. The hand-picked crew members began arriving at Scampton towards the end of March and all were curious as to why they were there. Some arrived as part of a complete crew; others found that they had been separated from their normal crews for various reasons, but they soon found themselves new crew members and all settled in quite quickly in spite of the problems of forming a new squadron in such a hurry.

Guy picked for his two Flight Commanders Squadron Leader H M Young, DFC and Squadron Leader H E Maudslay, DFC. Squadron Leader Young was a former Oxford rowing blue and had already completed two tours. He came from 57 Squadron. Twice he had had to ditch into the sea and this experience led to him being given the nickname of 'Dinghy'. Squadron Leader Maudslay was an old Etonian and arrived at the new squadron from 50 Squadron.

Guy was also pleased to have with him three pilots from 106 Squadron, Burpee, Shannon and, of course, his

Squadron Leader Melvin 'Dinghy' Young.

old friend 'Hoppy' Hopgood. Guy's own wireless operator, Flight Lieutenant Hutchison from 106 Squadron, rejoined him shortly after his arrival at Scampton. The Australian low-flying expert, Micky Martin, was also included, as was the tall blond American, Joe McCarthy. Other crews came from Australia, New Zealand and Canada.

From the start it became clear that many questions would be asked about the formation of this new squadron and that no answers would be given until the mission, for which they had been formed, had taken place. Guy, always a strict disciplinarian, now issued dire threats to anyone who spoke out of turn or breached any security regulations. He stressed how important it was to keep silent about what was happening at Scampton and, in truth, there was very little that could be said at that stage anyway. At the start even he was unaware of the target.

This omission was quickly rectified after Guy went down to Surrey to meet the man who would be providing the crews with the special weapon needed for this raid, Barnes Wallis. Barnes Wallis had been expecting to talk completely freely with the Wing Commander chosen to undertake this project and was amazed when he discovered that Guy had not been informed of the target. Guy's lack of information made it more difficult for the scientist to discuss the finer points of his invention, but he did show Guy a film of the trials that had already been carried out. For the first time Guy saw a film of the amazing weapon that his squadron would use: the bouncing bomb.

Shortly after his first meeting with Wallis, Guy was informed, by AVM Cochrane at No. 5 Group HQ in Grantham, that the target would be the dams of the

'Guy, always a strict disciplinarian, now issued dire threats to anyone who spoke out of turn or breached any security regulations.'

An original diagram showing a cross-section of the dam and the release point of the bomb.

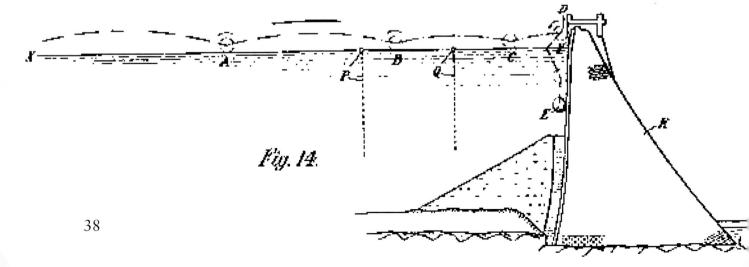

Fig. 14.

Ruhr, at the heart of Germany's industrial area.

Returning to visit Barnes Wallis at his office in Weybridge, Surrey, Guy was now able to discuss the project from an informed viewpoint and pilot and inventor set about the task of ironing out the difficulties that they would each, no doubt, encounter.

Back at Scampton the Squadron was training hard. Guy was still the only one to know the target, but he told the others enough for them to guess that the raid would be made over water and at a low level. Speculation was rife, the most popular view being that the target was either the *Tirpitz* or, perhaps, U-boat pens.

Whenever he was at Scampton Guy trained just as hard as the others, but much of his time was spent with administration work, planning the most daring raid yet to be undertaken by the RAF. His own crew found that they were flying every evening because it was generally the only time available to Guy for training. They decided that they didn't really mind as it kept them off the 'booze'.

Gibson was also involved with the trials still being carried out on the bomb which was code-named Upkeep. Security was so tight that whenever Guy went down to visit Barnes Wallis he used different modes of transport and different routes so that no one would know where he had been. Although the bomb worked in theory and small practice bombs had worked in reality, there were still a lot of tests to be carried out before Barnes Wallis was satisfied that it would work properly on the day. Many test drops were made at Chesil Beach in Dorset and at Reculver Bay in Kent. Whenever it was possible Guy attended these trials and, at first, witnessed the disappointing results, as the casings of the bombs broke up when they hit the water.

Barnes Wallis had asked Guy if it was possible for the pilots to fly the aircraft at a height of 150 feet and this they managed to do. However, when it became obvious that the casing was breaking each time because the bomb was being dropped from too great a height, Wallis revised his calculations and Guy was requested to fly at a height of 60 feet. Guy took this news back to his Squadron and they set about trying to devise a way of accurately measuring their height. The crews found that, during the day, this request was not too difficult to fulfil but at night, with the ground almost entirely obscured from view, it was practically impossible. Micky Martin was the expert on low flying, but even he did not have the answer. Aircraft were landing back at Scampton after low flying trials with bits of tree branches and leaves stuck in their undercarriages. The problem was even worse when flying over water as there was no way of judging the

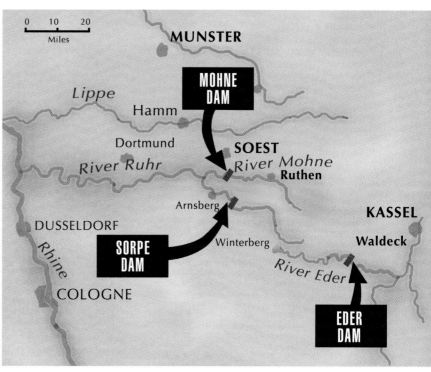

617 SQUADRON'S OBJECTIVES

height at all, but the problem was finally resolved by a man from the Ministry of Aircraft Production.

His solution was quite simple. He suggested that two lamps be fitted to the underside of the aircraft. If these were placed at the correct angle their beams would converge at the exact height that Barnes Wallis required.

Hurriedly the lamps were fitted to an aeroplane and it was sent off on a test flight. It worked and the problem had been solved.

For most of the crews training took place during the day as well as in the evening and there arose the problem of simulating moonlight whilst flying in daylight. Someone suggested using sunglasses but that did not work as it was almost impossible to see the instruments whilst wearing them. Then it was discovered that there was a system of simulating moonlight by painting the screens blue and wearing yellow goggles. Once again an aircraft was modified in this way and a successful test was carried out.

There remained a problem with navigation. Since tile aircraft would be flying really low, they would appear to be moving faster across the ground than if they were at a higher altitude. This meant that they would need large-scale maps and there arose the problem of how to cope with many maps during the flight without getting them all in a muddle. For some the answer was to stick them all together and then roll them. In this way the section already used could be wound up, leaving exposed the part currently being used.

A similar simple solution was found to the problem of

'Although the bomb worked in theory and small practice bombs had worked in reality, there were still a lot of tests to be carried out before Barnes Wallis was satisfied that it would work properly on the day.'

a suitable bomb sight. Not only did the aircraft have to be flown at a specific height but the bomb had to be dropped at an exact distance from the target. A bomb sight was made which meant that this was possible. It was a Y shaped device with pins on each of the open ends. When these were lined up with the towers on the dams the aircraft was the exact distance away from the target for the bomb to be dropped. Although this was a very simple device it did not suit all the bomb aimers in the Squadron and some of them made their own arrangements by drawing parallel lines on the clear panel in the nose of the aircraft.

While all these problems were being solved and the crews were perfecting their low-flying techniques at night, Guy was still very busy. The tests were still being carried out on the bomb and one day Guy took the Squadron bombing leader, an Australian Flight Lieutenant named Bob Hay, with him when he went to watch one of these tests in Kent. After it was over the two men climbed into their Magister to fly back to base. They had only been airborne for a few minutes when the engine cut out and Guy frantically searched for an empty field in which to land. This proved to be quite difficult as most of the available space had been made unserviceable by various devices such as poles and barbed wire in case of a German invasion. Eventually, however, he did manage to find a small piece of ground but the aeroplane crashed on landing. Luckily both Guy and Bob Hay were unhurt but were very amused when a man ran up to see if they were all right and, looking at them both, stated that he thought the RAF made people as young as they were fly too early.

As if a crash at this stage was not bad enough Guy had developed a carbuncle on the side of his face which was very painful. Using his oxygen mask made it even worse and he went to the doctor to see what could be done about it. The doctor said that he thought Guy had been working much too hard and that the carbuncle had appeared because he was run down. The solution was simple. He prescribed a complete rest for a couple of weeks. Guy could only laugh at this suggestion and put up with the pain and inconvenience.

Guy had very little relaxation at all during this period. Sometimes, when time permitted, he would go for long walks with his dog, Nigger. He had been given permission to use the grounds of a nearby country estate for these walks and sometimes he took Nigger out in a

Canadian pilot Flight Sergeant Ken Brown who, on the night of the raid, bombed the Sorpe dam.

'They had only been airborne for a few minutes when the engine cut out and Guy frantically searched for an empty field in which to land.'

boat on the lake which formed part of the estate. He enjoyed this time spent away from everyone as it gave him time to think without being distracted by the pressures of life on the Squadron. As he had discovered with his last command, it was sometimes a lonely job being a squadron commander. Although he had friends on the Squadron, there was really no one to whom he could turn without being accused of favouritism. So he began to regard Nigger as his best friend and the quiet moments he spent in the countryside with his dog were very precious to him.

When he did allow himself a few hours for a party, he always enjoyed himself, although, as Squadron Commander, he remained more sober than he had in the past. He liked nothing more than a riotous party but his work still came first; nothing was going to stop him from making the best possible job that he could of this assignment.

It has been said of Guy that he did not have anything to do with the NCOs on the Squadron. This was not true. He simply did not have much time or opportunity to mix with anyone. He had, however, discovered that two Squadron members were keen swimmers. These were the Canadian pilot Flight Sergeant Ken Brown and his English Flight Engineer, Sergeant Basil Feneron who, on the night of the raid, bombed the Sorpe dam. On a few occasions Guy accompanied them when they went into Lincoln to the swimming baths and was able to forget his responsibilities for an hour or two while they all messed about in the water. Guy was just as active in the horseplay as were the other two and on one occasion sneaked up behind Ken Brown, who was wearing a smart bathing robe that he had borrowed from Basil Feneron, and pushed him into the pool.

At the beginning of May Guy was dismayed to discover a serious breach in security. The armament officer, Pilot Officer H 'Doc' Watson, had spent three weeks at Mansion in Kent during April in connection with the bombing trials. When he returned to Scampton, he told Guy that three days after his arrival at Manston he had been shown a file which contained diagrams, maps and other secret details connected with the forthcoming raid. Guy was furious when he realized that Pilot Officer Watson knew more than either of the Flight Commanders did. In fact he knew more than Guy himself did at that stage. He was even more upset when he learned from Pilot Officer Watson that he was not

The specially adapted Lancaster releasing the oil drum shaped bomb. This was not the original design planned for the bomb by Wallis.

alone when this information had been given to him and that an officer from 618 Squadron had also been shown the file. Guy immediately had a very serious talk with Pilot Officer Watson and stressed the need for complete security. He then wrote a strong letter to the senior staff officer at HQ No. 5 Group in Grantham, explaining what had happened and pointing out that, in his opinion, it was completely unnecessary for an armament officer to have any of this information. Air Vice Marshal Cochrane, AOC No. 5 Group, agreed with Guy and the officer who had shown Pilot Officer Watson the file had it removed from his charge, and was severely reprimanded for putting the security of the entire operation in jeopardy.

The flying training continued during the first part of May without any mishaps. The only people who really felt they were suffering were the local farmers. A number of them considered that the Squadron's low-level flying, was disturbing their animals and some complaints were received at Scampton. Nevertheless the low-level flying continued. Much of it was done over water at Uppingham Lake, Colchester Reservoir and the Derwent Dam.

Gradually the numerous problems were ironed out and there remained only the problem of the bomb itself. After a number of tests, these problems were also resolved: the actual bomb used on the raid was slightly different in appearance from the one first envisaged by Barnes Wallis. The outer casing, which kept breaking, was removed and the finished bomb looked something like a large oil drum. Since it was of an unconventional shape and size it was

'In addition to its size and shape, the bomb was also unique in that, to perform correctly, it needed to be spun backwards before being released.'

not possible to carry it in the bomb bay and it had to be slung under the aircraft, which had to be adapted. In addition to its size and shape, the bomb was also unique in that, to perform correctly, it needed to be spun backwards before being released. The equipment that was needed for this task had also to be housed in the adapted aircraft.

The date set for the raid on the dams was around 19 May, 1943. This depended on the level of the water in the reservoirs and photo-reconnaissance aircraft had been regularly sent out to photograph the dams in the weeks leading up to the raid. The crews were briefed to ascertain the water level and to note any changes being made at the dams, so ensuring that the Germans were not expecting an attack. There was a moment of concern when it was discovered that the Germans had placed some tall, pointed objects along the top of the Möhne dam, but these were later found to be ornamental conifers used to beautify rather than defend the structure.

Although the day was fast approaching when the raid would be carried out, the men of 57 Squadron were beginning to wonder if 617 Squadron would ever do anything. They had spent such a lot of time training while the other Squadron at Scampton had been making many operational flights, so it was not surprising that they were teased for being armchair pilots. Very soon, however, that all changed.

Micky Martin, recalling the week before the raid, remembered how they all tried to fit in as much living as possible during that week. Although they had not been told what the target would be, they all knew that it was

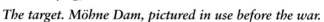

The target. Möhne Dam, pictured in use before the war.

a very special raid and most believed that it would be so dangerous that the chances of returning were probably quite slim. In these circumstances it seemed a shame to leave anything undone and even more of a waste to leave any money unspent. Guy himself spent some money that week in buying a birthday present of a gold and enamel brooch for his young cousin Janet. He never forgot her at Christmas time or on her birthday and had no intentions of doing so now, just because he had only one week to go before the raid. Janet was thrilled to receive the gift, her first piece of real jewellery, for her ninth birthday.

Unlike his crews. Guy knew, rather than surmised, that the target would be a dangerous one. It was obvious that the dams were very important to the Germans and they would not let them be destroyed without a good fight. Worse still for Guy was the fact that he would be leading the raid and would be the first to discover just how strong these defences were.

Even when he was given the date of the raid as the night of Sunday, 16 May Guy could not relax for a moment. There were still little last minute problems which occurred and he had to write out the operation order in great detail. This task was completed on 15 May, the day after the full dress rehearsal at Uppingham Lake when Guy was accompanied by the Station Commander, Group Captain Whitworth. It was a complete success.

Since it had been decided that Guy would co-ordinate the entire operation by radio, one of the first instances of using a 'Master bomber', certain code words were devised to simplify the procedure. Words such as 'Dinghy' and 'Nigger' would signify that the targets had been destroyed.

It was, perhaps, a horrible irony that the word 'Nigger' should have been chosen to mean the destruction of a target, for, on the night of 15 May as Guy was writing out his operation orders, his beloved dog, Nigger, was killed by a car outside the main gates at Scampton. Group Captain Whitworth brought Guy the awful news and told him that Nigger's body had been brought into the guard room.

It is not hard to imagine how Guy must have felt at that moment. Nigger had been his faithful companion since he first came to live with him as a puppy down in Kent. They had shared so much and, when times were hard for Guy, Nigger had always been there with a friendly greeting for his master. The dog's death was a

Guy and his crew climbing aboard their Lancaster before leaving to bomb the Möhne Dam.

'When the time came to leave, there was great excitement and almost the entire station turned out to wave 617 on their way.'

devastating blow for Guy, and coming, as it did, the day before the most important mission he had ever flown, was a disaster. He was, however, a true professional in his work and was determined not to let this personal tragedy affect the raid. His time for grieving would have to wait until the raid had been satisfactorily carried out. Knowing that some of the crews might regard Nigger's death as a bad omen, Guy asked that they should not be told until after their return.

The next morning Guy arranged the burial of his dog. He did not want to do it himself but asked that it be carried out at midnight that night, which was the time he was due to be over the target. He spoke to a Flight Sergeant in the station workshop and asked him to build a coffin for Nigger but the man refused and a row ensued. Guy, perhaps understandably, completely lost his temper, but did not get the coffin for his dog. He left the details of the burial to Flight Sergeant Powell, 617's disciplinary NCO. The burial was carried out exactly as Guy had requested, and at midnight his little friend was laid to rest. Marked much later by a proper stone, the carefully tended little grave remains to this day on the grass outside the original 617 Squadron offices at RAF Scampton.

Sunday, 16 May was a hot day and the forecast for the raid remained good. During the day the crews were told what their targets would be and they spent some hours examining the models of the dams and fixing the details in their minds.

When the time came to leave, there was great excitement and almost the entire station turned out to wave 617 on their way. As Guy was climbing into his Lancaster a photographer drove up to take a photo of the departing crew. Guy, in shirt-sleeves, stopped at the top of the ladder and turned. His crew, still on the ground, turned also and the photo was taken. Guy told the photographer that 'just in case' he had better send a copy to his wife and his crew laughed. As they disappeared into the aircraft, their laughter could still be heard. They obviously thought Guy's statement to be ridiculous. They would be coming back; there was no doubt about that in the minds of any of them.

Guy in his Lancaster, AJ-G, took off at 21.39 hours accompanied by Hoppy Hopgood in AJ-M and Micky Martin in AJ-P. They were followed minutes later by six more aircraft, including those of the two Flight Commanders. These nine aircraft would make the attack on the main targets of the Möhne and Eder dams. Then came five more crews heading for the Sorpe dam. The remaining aircraft, out of the total of nineteen, would be used wherever they were needed and could be contacted by radio to be given their orders.

Much has been written about the raid and its consequences. It was, of course, a great success, although in terms of crews lost it was an expensive operation. Of the nineteen aircraft which left Scampton that May evening only eleven were to return. From the eight aircraft lost, only three men would survive.

The outward flight for Guy and his two companions was relatively peaceful, at least until they reached the Dutch coast. As they approached the Möhne dam they flew over the Rhine and down towards the Möhne Lake which was calm and still and looked like a mirror in the moonlight.

Guy made a dummy run over the dam and then came in to line up for his attack. The flak was quite heavy but the attack was successfully made and the aircraft was not damaged. The bomb dropped in the correct place and as it exploded a huge wall of water was thrown into the night air. It took several minutes for the spray to subside and when it did the dam was seen to be still intact.

Guy then called in Hoppy to make his run. As he approached the wall his aircraft was hit and his bomb was released a little too late. Instead of bouncing up to the dam wall and then sinking it dropped over the top of the dam and landed on a power station on the other side, exploding immediately. This explosion may have destroyed one of the flak guns. Hoppy called for the crew to bale out and tried to climb while they were doing so to give them a better chance of survival. It was no good. Only two members of the crew managed to bale out and live to tell the tale. A third left the aircraft, but did not survive the fall. Seconds later the aircraft crashed

'Guy then called in Hoppy to make his run. As he approached the wall his aircraft was hit and his bomb was released a little too late. Instead of bouncing up to the dam wall and then sinking it dropped over the top of the dam and landed on a power station on the other side, exploding immediately.'

Above & below: The aftermath. Pictures taken by the Germans and the RAF show the true extent of the bomb damage.

with shooting down AJ-M was not killed. He was Corporal Karl Schutte, 23-year-old commander of the North Tower flak gun, who survived the attack to be decorated, a week later, with the Iron Cross, 2nd class.

It took two more bombs before the dam was finally breached by the one dropped from David Maltby's aircraft. As each aircraft made their bombing run Guy flew alongside diverting the flak. Then on they went to the Eder dam where Guy, once more, directed the attack. After it was hit by the third bomb, delivered by Les Knight and his crew, the Eder dam also collapsed with a huge hole across its middle. It had not been necessary to use diversionary tactics at this dam. There were no flak positions on its walls as there had been at the Möhne. The Eder dam was in a difficult position to reach at low level with a large aircraft and the Germans had obviously thought an attack to be impossible. They had not reckoned with the tenacity of the men of 617 Squadron.

The return journey was filled with a mixture of elation and sadness. The task had been completed but at what cost. In a misspelt entry in his logbook Guy said simply of the raid;

'Led attack on Möhne an[d] Eder dams. Successful.'

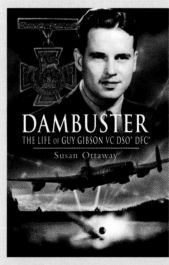

with a huge explosion and the subsequent fire burned for a long time, a constant reminder to the other crews of the dangers they were facing.

Guy, circling around and watching this, was helpless to do anything. He told his uncle and aunt later that when he saw his friend shot down something inside him snapped and all he could think of was to get whoever had been responsible for Hoppy's death.

As he called Micky Martin in to make the third attack, Guy decided to fly along with him in order to try to divert the flak from the attacking aircraft to his own. This worked and although Martin's aircraft was hit he was able to make a successful attack and, ultimately, return to England.

When Guy flew in alongside the other aircraft, the gunners in AJ-G fired furiously at the gun emplacements on the dam. In spite of their efforts the man credited

'There was a muffled explosion and when the spray had cleared a bit I had a quick look over the parapet down at the dam wall and shouted, "The wall's had it."'

Unteroffizier Karl Schutte

46

DIGITAL RECONSTRUCTION: JON WILKINSON

BREAKING THE DAMS: THE STORY OF DAMBUSTER DAVID MALTBY AND HIS CREW

Four of the five aircraft in the second wave took off first (Joe McCarthy found a fault in his plane and had to transfer to the reserve, which led him to be delayed). It wasn't common for Lancasters to take off in formation but on this occasion they did; Gibson leading Hopgood and Martin down the grass runway into the bright May evening sky.

By Charles Foster

This article was extracted from Breaking The Dams - The Story of Dambuster David Maltby and His Crew and is reproduced here by permission of Pen and Sword Books Ltd.

At 2147 on 16 May 1943, Young led out the V-Vic with the two Davids just behind; Maltby on the right, Shannon on the left. Sitting at his desk inside the fuselage, below the Perspex astrodome, with his maps, an air position indicator and the apparatus for the Gee system at hand, Vivian Nicholson sat ready for his first ever operation.

The navigator would spend the whole flight making detailed calculations and advising small changes in course and the Gee system was there to help him. Introduced in 1942, Gee sent out pulses from three separate transmitters, located in southern England, which appeared as blips on a screen in front of the navigator. It was designed to make it easier for him to get an accurate fix of the aircraft's position. However, it had limited range and the signal was frequently jammed by the Germans, so it was not always useful. That was certainly the case on the night of the Dams Raid.

Vivian's log records the details of the flight. At 2210, over the Wash, they tested the spotlights set to keep the aircraft at exactly 60ft during the bombing run. They made landfall accurately over the Scheldt estuary on the Dutch coast at 2312, and the mine was then fused. David had to take 'evasive action' to avoid flak at Rosendaal. At the canal intersection at Beck, Vivian wrote '*Leader turns soon*'. He probably meant 'too soon', as Young's aircraft went slightly off course. At 2342, about 15 miles from the Rhine, he noted that his Gee system was now 'jammed something chronic'. They turned again at Dülmen, avoided more flak, 'direct at a/c' at Ludinghausen, and also at Ahlen, and arrived at Target X, the Möhne at 0026. The outward flight had taken 2 hours 32 minutes.

It had been a textbook flight out. Major Alan Thompson, an Army pilot who now conducts tours around Dambuster sites for a travel company, says that he always describes the crew of AJ-J as doing the job exactly as they had been instructed. They stayed low, took evasive action when necessary and hit all their turning points accurately. And, of course, in a few minutes they would drop their mine at the right height, the right distance and the right speed.

David Maltby and Guy Gibson in the Squadron CO's office at RAF Scampton. Taken in July 1943. IWM/TR1122

David Maltby at the controls of an Avro Manchester, the unloved and unreliable precursor of the Lancaster. Probably taken in the autumn of 1941. J T KOVASCO/GARBETT GOULDING COLLECTION

But that was to come. For the moment David and the other five crews circled the area above the Möhne, to be joined shortly by Maudslay and Knight. Bill Astell had crashed. He seems to have hesitated at a turning point, then flew into flak and collided with a high tension pylon. His crew included two Canadians, Albert Garshowitz and Frank Garbas, who had grown up together as friends in Hamilton, Ontario, and are now buried together in Reichswald Forest Cemetery.

The Möhne Reservoir is the shape of a giant U on its side, the open end facing east, or right. The dam is on the top left part of the curve of the U. Earlier books, including Sweetman's, say that the aircraft approached from the Korbecke bridge at the eastern end, but that is now thought to be wrong. The aircraft attacked by flying straight at the dam from a south-easterly direction, hopping over a small spit of land and quickly getting down to the right height for the last stretch of about 1,500m. In that last 1,500m the pilot would have to get down to exactly 60 ft and stay level, the flight engineer would maintain the approach speed at 230 mph, and the wireless operator would ensure that the mine was spinning backwards at 500 rpm. Meanwhile the navigator would switch on the spotlights and check that the beams were touching. Flying at 230 mph, the aircraft would cover the 1,500m stretch in about 15 seconds.

> '*By the time Young, Maltby and Shannon had got to the dam Gibson had flown over it, without revealing the exact direction of attack, and come through the flak unscathed.*'

It is not always noted that Chastise marked another important innovation in bombing technique. VHF radio sets, previously only fitted to fighter aircraft, were used for the first time on this raid. This meant that crews could talk to each other and therefore be controlled by a leader, or 'master bomber' as they were later to be known.

By the time Young, Maltby and Shannon had got to the dam Gibson had flown over it, without revealing the exact direction of attack, and come through the flak unscathed. He told the others that he '*liked the look of it*'. So, just two minutes after this trio arrived, he began his run in. It seemed at first that everything had gone to plan – the mine was spun correctly and was seen to bounce three times. But it did not reach the dam wall, exploding a few yards short. A great plume of water rose up into the air, but the dam held.

Back in Britain, in the operations room at 5 Group headquarters in Grantham, Wallis, Cochrane and other assorted staff had been joined by Air Marshal Sir Arthur Harris himself, who had driven the 120 miles from Bomber Command HQ in High Wycombe. When Gibson's '*Goner 58A*' signal was received, indicating an unsuccessful attack – the mine had exploded between 5-50 yards short – a sense of gloom descended.

Gibson then called Hopgood into attack. Flt Sgt John Fraser, Hopgood's bomb aimer, later remembered

Gibson describing the run-in as a *'piece of cake'*, which is certainly not what it seemed like to him. (How frightfully understated the slang of that time seems to us today.) As Hopgood crossed the stretch of water towards the dam, the anti-aircraft gunners on it were now ready. His aircraft was hit on one side. The flight engineer shouted a warning, Fraser dropped the mine, knowing that he had done so too late and heard Hopgood screaming *'For Christ's sake get out of here!'* Hopgood struggled on, trying to lift the aircraft, and got it up to about 500 ft. The mine bounced over the dam and into the power station on the far side, causing a big explosion and a fire. Fraser, Minchin and Burcher, baled out but Minchin, already injured, did not survive the parachute drop. Hopgood and the other three died in the crash. Burcher and Fraser were captured. Fraser went back to Canada after the war; later he would name his first son John Hopgood Fraser after the pilot who had kept his aircraft aloft long enough to save his life.

John Fort, in his 617 Squadron days. PETER FORT/ALEX BATEMAN

The next few minutes were surely what earned Gibson his Victoria Cross, as he called up Martin to attack. In the words of John Sweetman:

> *'Gibson's leadership and Martin's courage ensured that the operation would not disintegrate.'*

Gibson flew slightly ahead of Martin on his starboard side, in the hope that the gunners would be distracted. However, something went wrong with Martin's mine: it veered off to the left and exploded near the southern shore of the lake. Its casing may have been damaged when it was dropped accidentally onto the hard standing at Scampton that morning, or, perhaps, Martin hadn't got the aircraft exactly level as it was released.

Sqn Ldr Melvin Young, whose rowing Blue from Oxford may have helped him survive the two ditchings at sea which earned him the nickname 'Dinghy', was next. This time, Gibson flew across the defences on the far side of the dam wall, and Martin came in on the starboard side. Young was accurate in his approach, and his bomb aimer, Fg Off Vincent MacCausland, dropped the mine accurately. It bounced three times, hit the dam and seemed to explode while it was in contact with it, but, as the tumult subsided, there was no obvious breach.

As they waited, knowing they were next in, David and his crew continued to circle north of the dam, along with the aircraft of Shannon, Maudslay and Knight. Vivian Nicholson noted 'flak none too light'. Gibson told David to go ahead at 0048, and Vivian wrote, 'received OK' as they started the approach. This time, three Lancasters flew towards the target. Gibson on David's starboard side, Martin over to port.

Anthony Stone checked the spinning mine, John Fort lay flat on his stomach in the front fuselage, with Vic Hill's feet planted in their stirrups over his head. As they came over the spit of land, Vivian turned on the spotlights and peered out of the starboard blister at the beams, calling, 'Down, down' as their lights came closer and closer. Up in the cockpit, in the left-hand seat, David adjusted the height and kept the aircraft level while, next to him, Bill Hatton watched the speed and moved the throttles. As they approached the dam wall, David suddenly realised that from this close he could see a small breach had occurred in the centre and that there was crumbling along the crown. Young's mine had been successful

William Hatton. Photograph probably taken in late 1942, as he is wearing his Flight Engineer's brevet. GUY VOICE

Antony Stone in about 1942, soon after qualifying as a Wireless Operator/Air Gunner.

GARBETT/GOULDING COLLECTION

Harold Simmonds in 1942, wearing his trainee forage cap with white flash.

GRACE BLACKBURN

after all! In a last second change of plan he veered slightly to port but stayed dead level as John Fort steadied himself to press the release. The mine bounced four times and struck the wall. Over the dam they flew, now turning hard left, Harold Simmonds in the rear turret firing on the gun emplacements that were still active.

The dam was protected by a flak battery in each of the two sluice towers and another in the wall. In the northern tower was a gunner called Unteroffizier Karl Schütte, who later wrote an account of the night's proceedings. In fact the flak guns in the north tower had jammed and Karl Schütte and his comrades were reduced to shooting at David's plane with rifles. The gun on the parapet was still firing, however. There are two slightly different versions of his account, one says:

> *'During the fourth attack, our gun failed after a premature explosion in the barrel. We bashed away with all our strength trying to clear the jam with a hammer and a metal spike but it was no good. When it came to the fifth attack we did what we'd so often done in training – let loose with our carbines. There was just one flak gun on the road still firing at the aircraft – now they had it all their own way. There was a muffled explosion and when the spray had cleared a bit I had a quick look over the parapet down at the*

> **'During the fourth attack, our gun failed after a premature explosion in the barrel. We bashed away with all our strength trying to clear the jam with a hammer and a metal spike but it was no good.'**

> *dam wall and shouted, 'The wall's had it.' The gunners didn't want to believe it at first but the breach got visibly bigger.'*

Another version says:

> *Then a fifth plane started its attack. Only the gun in the lower wall was still firing. The machine neared the wall at an incredible speed; they now had an easy game – I could almost touch it, yet I think even today I can see the outline of the pilot.*

It wasn't yet obvious whether the attack had been successful so at 0050 Antony Stone, doing his job correctly, radioed *'Goner 78A'* back to Grantham. ('Goner' meant a successful attack, '7' an explosion in contact with the dam, '8' no apparent breach, 'A' the target was the Möhne.)

David recorded afterwards that:

> *'Our load sent up water and mud to a height of a 1,000 ft. The spout of water was silhouetted against the moon. It rose with tremendous speed and then gently fell back. You could see the shock wave at the base of the jet.'*

> *'Bomb dropped. Wizard.'* was Vivian's more brief summary of the events.

The lake began to calm down again and Gibson called Shannon into the attack. But as Shannon began to line up the circling crews realised that the dam had indeed been broken. David's mine, dropped to the left of Young's, had been pulled towards it by the flow of water before it exploded and caused a second breach. (In the end the two breaches would be joined together by the force of escaping water to make a single breach some 76m wide.) It was 0056, a full six minutes after David's attack when the breach was confirmed. Gibson's wireless operator, Flt Lt Bob Hutchison, quickly tapped out the code word 'Nigger' and sent it back to Grantham.

So who actually broke the dam, Young or Maltby? As children, we were always told that David dropped the bomb that caused the breach. This impression is certainly given in the Gibson and Brickhill books and the 1955 film. In *Enemy Coast Ahead*, Gibson wrote that when Melvin Young said, *'I think I've done it, I've broken it'*, he told him he hadn't. To David's credit, he never claimed the breach as entirely his work – his answer to the debriefing questionnaire quite clearly states that as he attacked he saw the small breach made by Young, and that's why he turned slightly to port. Whether Young's small breach on its own would have resulted in a complete collapse of the dam is something that will never be known. The dam was immensely strong and it may well have needed two explosions to break it. What is quite clear is that only two mines out of the five were dropped correctly, and between them they broke the dam. Wallis' calculations were proven to be good.

The operations room at Grantham, in the basement of a large house called St Vincent's on the edge of the town, was accurately reproduced in the 1955 film. It was a long narrow room, with a raised platform down one side where the chief signals officer, Wg Cdr Wally Dunn, sat anxiously with a telephone plugged into the W/T Morse code receiver. Dunn could read Morse as quickly as any wireless operator and translated each message immediately to the group clustered in front of him, expectantly waiting.

There are two different versions of the timings of the four 'Goner' messages that were received from the Möhne. Both say that the first was Gibson's at 0037 and that then, for some reason, Young's arrived next at 0050, causing consternation amongst Satterly, Cochrane and others who knew the bombing order. This implied that only two of the first four aircraft had got through, and spelled disaster.

Wallis paced up and down, 'having kittens' according to Cochrane afterwards. Gibson's 'Goner' signal caused him to mutter, 'No, it's no good.' Young's made him bury his head in his hands. At 0050, when Antony Stone sent AJ-J's message, desperation set in, compounded by the late arrival at 0051 of Martin's. (The second version of the signal log shows that AJ-J's message was received at 0055, after Martin's was received at 0053.) Whichever order the signals were received in, back at Grantham it was thought that five aircraft had apparently failed. Nothing more was heard for perhaps as long as five minutes. But then, suddenly, at 0056, the 'Nigger' signal was received, and then confirmed.

Scenes of jubilation followed. Wallis leapt into the air, arms aloft. As Harris shook his hand, everyone who heard him remembers the words:

> 'Wallis, I didn't believe a word you said when you came to see me. But now you could sell me a pink elephant.'

At the Möhne the seven aircraft still aloft circled for a short while, chattering amongst themselves on the VHF sets. Then Gibson, conscious that they had only attacked the first of the night's targets, ordered the three that had still not bombed, Shannon, Maudslay and Knight, to accompany him and Young to the Eder. (Young was to act as his deputy if he went down.) He told David and Mick Martin to set course for home. At 0053.5, according to the meticulous Vivian, AJ-J set a bearing of 280 degrees and

> '**Wallis, I didn't believe a word you said when you came to see me. But now you could sell me a pink elephant.**'

headed off. The details are recorded again, turning points at Ahlen and Zutphen, with evasive action taken at Ahlen. They crossed the coast exactly one hour after leaving the Möhne, meeting some flak and searchlights there and with the Gee 'still no dice'. Crossing the North Sea, the Gee rather belatedly became 'faint but workable'. They rose to the giddy height of 1,500 ft, but then, somewhat oddly, descended again to test their spotlights. They crossed the bombing range at Wainfleet in the Wash, and touched down at Scampton at 0311. Martin's aircraft arrived safely eight minutes later.

There to greet them were Leading Aircraftmen Law and Payne. Once the aircraft had been handed over to the groundcrew, David and his colleagues went to stow their kit before meeting the intelligence officers for their

An aerial reconnaissance photograph of the Eder dam, taken in May 1943, before the attack.

EDER DAM
(before attack)
K 1559
Neg Nº 24687

debriefing. By the time Maltby bumped into Harry Humphries, Gibson and the Eder dam survivors must also have landed, as David was able to give Humphries news of some of the other casualties. Humphries remembers their conversation:

'How was it Dave?' I queried.

'A terrific show, Adj., absolutely terrific. I have never seen anything like it in my life,' he said, then quite bluntly, 'Hoppy's bought it.'

'Bought it, when?' I asked.

'Shot down over the target, and I am afraid we have lost several others too,' he answered. He pushed his Mae West viciously into his locker. 'Some didn't even get there and I am sure "Dinghy" Young got into trouble, and maybe Henry Maudsley [sic].'

He turned and gave me his usual broad grin. 'We pranged it though, Adj., oh boy did we prang it! Water, water everywhere. "Gibby" was

> **"'A terrific show, Adj., absolutely terrific. I have never seen anything like it in my life,' he said, then quite bluntly, 'Hoppy's bought it.'"**

everywhere. How the hell the Jerry gunners missed him I don't know.' He added, 'Did you bury "Nigger" for the Wingco?'

I started, 'I um.. to tell you the truth, Dave, I don't know. Why do you ask anyway?'

'Oh it was just worrying Gibby, I know. It just struck me that superstition means nothing anyway, even though I always take this hat with me.'

'This hat' was David's field service or 'fore and aft'. It was a filthy thing, covered in oil and grease but he would not be separated from that hat, even on parade. 'Well, see you later over a beer,' he said and shouted to the rest of his crew, 'so long sprogs, thanks for coming.'

It is likely that this conversation occurred after the crews had been debriefed, with an intelligence officer giving all the pilots a questionnaire and recording their comments. In it, David described how he saw a breach in the centre of the dam before attacking, and

Battle order for Operation Chastise, called 'Night Flying Programme' for security reasons. The aircraft piloted by Hopgood, Young, Maudslay, Astell, Byers, Barlow, Ottley and Burpee did not return. Only three of the 56 airmen in these eight crews survived. LINCOLNSHIRE COUNTY COUNCIL, GRANTHAM MUSEUM

went to port and made a contact. His mine was spun correctly and bounced three times. His main criticism was that the aircraft were exposed by being against the moon as they made their attack.

By 0400, Harris, Cochrane and Wallis had all left Grantham for Scampton, and personally greeted some of the later arrivals. The last aircraft to get back – at 0615 – was piloted by Bill Townsend, who did not recognise Harris in his Air Chief Marshal's uniform and pushed past him rather abruptly.

By then, the knowledge of who had not survived must have begun to sink in. David had seen Hopgood shot down, and would have known that Astell had never got as far as the target. With Young and Maudslay failing to make it back from the Eder, four of the elite nine in the first wave had gone. From the second and third waves, another four crews – Barlow, Byers, Ottley and Burpee – had been lost. Like David, Lewis Burpee had a pregnant wife waiting at home.

It is not certain, but it is unlikely that, in the dawn light, David travelled the 30 miles back to Woodhall Spa to see his own pregnant wife. By all accounts he was an

> 'With only eleven of the nineteen Lancasters having returned, the airfield seemed a lot quieter.'

enthusiastic party-goer and would have joined in the general merriment that ensued amongst many of the survivors. The mess bars were reopened, and Group Captain Whitworth's house became the scene of an impromptu party, culminating in a conga dance around his house and the seizing of his pyjamas as a trophy. In any event, David was certainly at Scampton some time in the morning, since he is in the photograph taken outside the officers' mess. When this was taken, apparently, many of those photographed were somewhat the worse for wear, though it is not too obvious from the picture.

With only eleven of the nineteen Lancasters having returned, the airfield seemed a lot quieter. A Tannoy announcement during the morning told everyone on the base what had occurred, but many were more aware of the scale of the losses. At one point Wallis was reported to be in tears, devastated by the fact that fifty-six young men were missing. (At that stage no one knew that three had survived and been captured as prisoners of war.) Although the last scene of the 1955 film, where Gibson and Wallis have a conversation which ends with Gibson saying, 'I have

A group of Dams Raid survivors outside the Officers' Mess on the morning of 17 May 1943. As most had been drinking hard since soon after they landed they look surprisingly spruce. John Fort is on the extreme right in the front row, David Maltby second from right in the second row. IWM/HU91948

some letters to write', is fictionalised, it bears some, but not complete, resemblance to the truth. It was Humphries and Sgt Heveron who spent much of the morning sending telegrams to the next of kin. In the afternoon, they were interrupted by Gibson, bearing the news that all 900 aircrew and groundcrew were to be sent on leave the next day. The process of drafting letters to the next of kin didn't begin until Tuesday 18 May, after the leave had begun.

By that time, the world had been informed of the scale of the achievement. BBC radio had broadcast the Air Ministry communiqué at lunchtime on the Monday. (The same communiqué was read again for the 1955 film by the wartime BBC announcer Frank Phillips, where, as the words die away, we see a moving set of shots including the survivors eating breakfast, the empty chairs in the mess, Dinghy Young's Oxford oar on the wall and an alarm clock ticking away, its hands showing the time as just after 6.00am. It is a beautiful, understated piece of visual and sound editing, and another occasion where the scriptwriter and director's decisions to vary the historical record slightly by bringing the broadcast forward in time by several hours is fully justified.)

This is London. The Air Ministry has just issued the following communiqué. In the early hours of this morning, a force of Lancasters of Bomber Command led by Wing Cdr G P Gibson DSO DFC attacked with mines the dams of the Möhne and Sorpe reservoirs. These control over two-thirds of the water storage capacity of the Ruhr basin. Reconnaissance later established that the Möhne dam had been breached over a length of one hundred yards, and that the power station below had been swept away. The Eder dam, which controls the headwaters of the Weser and Fulde valleys and operates several power stations, was also attacked and reported as breached. Photographs show the river below the dam in full flood. The attacks were pressed home from a very low level with great determination and coolness in the face of fierce resistance. Eight of the Lancasters are missing.

On the Tuesday, every paper carried the full story as its lead. David found time to let his family know that he had been involved. He sent a telegram to his uncle, Aubrey Hatfeild, who had been a pilot in the RFC in the First World War: 'We let the plug out!' In his diary, Ettrick recorded that David had 'returned first from the Möhne Dam'.

Scampton, 27 May 1943. The crews were presented to the King and Queen in their bombing order. David Maltby stands before the King, with his pocket bulging with a tobacco pouch and other smoking equipment. WM CH9929/CH9953

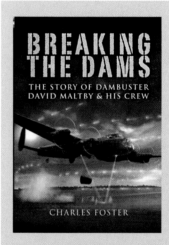

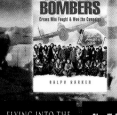

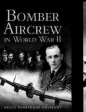

'Young's weapon made three good bounces and contact. It sank to its preset depth and exploded against the dam wall as Wallis had predicted. Another huge column of water rose and a shock wave could be seen rippling through the lake '

56

DAMBUSTER WHO CRACKED THE DAM: THE STORY OF MELVIN 'DINGHY' YOUNG

When Melvin Young left the USA at the beginning of February 1943 he did not know what fate and the RAF had in store for him, except that he expected, and wanted, to return to operational flying. The climax of his life which now unfolded saw him take a central role in arguably the most famous single action of the RAF, Operation *Chastise*. Sadly, it was to cost his life and the lives of fifty-two other young flyers.

By Arthur G Thorning

This article was extracted from *The Dambuster Who Cracked the Dam* and is reproduced here by permission of Pen and Sword Books Ltd.

It seems likely that Melvin met his crew at 1660 CU at Swinderby. The 1660 Conversion Unit (CU) Operational Record Book (ORB) shows that five of them (Horsfall, Beesley, Nichols, Yeo and Ibbotson) had flown together on an operation to Berlin on 16/17 January, with Pilot Officer V Duxbury DFC as pilot and Flight Lieutenant T W Blair as navigator. Some nineteen aircraft from various CUs were detailed to attack Berlin, but for technical reasons only three, including the above crew, succeeded – bombs were aimed at red markers laid by Pathfinder aircraft and were seen to burst across these 'red cascades'. The flak over the target was heavy but inaccurate.

The following night David Horsfall flew with Flying Officer H W Southgate on another raid to Berlin, when they bombed an estimated position over solid cloud cover. Horsfall would have gained some useful experience since the return flight from the Dutch coast was made on three engines 'as the starboard inner cut'.

Melvin's original crew were all sergeants:

David Horsfall – flight engineer
Charles Roberts – navigator
Lawrence Nichols – wireless operator
Gordon Yeo – air gunner
Wilfred Ibbotson – air gunner.

The original bomb aimer was probably John Beesley, but for some reason he was judged unsuitable for 617 Squadron and a Canadian, Flying Officer Vincent MacCausland, was drafted into the crew. Beesley was later shot down on a raid with another squadron and became a prisoner of war.

On 13 March Melvin and his new crew were posted to 57 Squadron at Scampton, a pre-war RAF aerodrome with the usual complement of permanent buildings, four

Squadron Leader Melvin 'Dinghy' Young RAFVR, DFC and Bar. This portrait photograph was taken in the USA in 1942 and sent to his mother on her birthday.

miles north of Lincoln. Coincidentally, the Station Commander at Scampton was Group Captain J N H 'Charles' Whitworth, who had been Melvin's flying instructor in the Oxford University Air Squadron. Before Melvin could take part in any operations with 57 Squadron he was caught up in the urgent formation of a new squadron which was to undertake a special operation and then be available for other unusual bombing tasks. For some years pre-war the RAF's strategic planners had determined that the destruction of the large dams supplying water to the Ruhr Valley steel industry might have a very great effect on German war production – many tons of water are required to produce a ton of steel. Also the consequent flooding would do a lot of damage and some hydro-electric power would be lost. There were several dams supplying the Ruhr, of which the Möhne Dam was the most important. This dam was, and indeed still is, having been rebuilt, an imposing, massive structure. To hit it with a sufficiently large, well-aimed conventional bomb dropped from high altitude was beyond the technology then available. Various ingenious alternative ways of attacking the dams were put forward but none showed much promise until Dr Barnes Wallis, of Vickers-Armstrong Ltd and designer of the Wellington bomber, devised a system for skipping a large depth charge along the surface of the water, thus clearing the anti-torpedo nets defending the water face of the dam. This would then hit the dam, roll down in contact with the wall and detonate three tons of high explosive thirty feet down. The water would concentrate the shock wave on the masonry and cause it to collapse.

This system was, of course, specifically designed to attack masonry dams of which there were several in the Ruhr area. However, the second most important dam serving the Ruhr was the Sorpe; this was of a later type with shallow sloping earth faces on each side of a concrete core, for which the weapon was not ideal, albeit it was to be used with a different technique. In the event the planners decided to make the second priority target the Eder Dam, some forty-six miles south-east of the Möhne. This was also a large masonry, gravity dam and held back the water of the largest reservoir in Germany. It did not supply the Ruhr industry but its destruction would do much flood damage and reinforce the message that Bomber Command could make devastating precision strikes. Other, less important, targets on the list for attack were the Lister, Diemeland Ennepe Dams.

Sir Charles Portal, the Chief of the Air Staff.

Air Vice Marshal The Hon. Sir Ralph Cochrane.

A series of experiments and flight trials produced a plan which required this weapon, code-named Upkeep, to be released under quite specific circumstances; about 450 yards from the dam, at 220 mph and at 60 feet above the water. The weapon, which was a cylinder carried under specially modified Lancasters, was to be spun backwards to aid the skipping process and help to keep it in contact with the water face of the dam as it sank to its detonation depth. All this is easily written but not easily achieved and the idea received much scepticism, not least from Air Marshal Sir Arthur 'Bomber' Harris, Commander-in-Chief of Bomber Command. However Sir Charles Portal, the Chief of the Air Staff was in favour of trying to break the dams, not least because it would be a great boost to morale and to Britain's standing with her allies, being able to mount a precision blow on a notable target. Thus a special Squadron was to be set up within 5 Group, Bomber Command, under the command of Air Vice Marshal The Hon Sir Ralph Cochrane, to make this attack.

The timescale was short, less than two months, since the lakes would be full in mid-May when a full moon would enable the crews to have a good chance of success. The operation would be flown at the lowest possible height to reduce the risk of being identified by radar and intercepted by night fighters.

The new squadron was soon allocated the now famous number 617; still a leading strike squadron in the RAF. The man designated by Harris to command the squadron and lead the attack was Wing Commander Guy Penrose Gibson.

> '...Sir Charles Portal, the Chief of the Air Staff was in favour of trying to break the dams, not least because it would be a great boost to morale and to Britain's standing with her allies...'

PERSONNEL

The plan for recruiting aircrew personnel for 617 Squadron was that, as far as possible, they should be from within 5 Group and should be from crews who had completed two operational tours. In practice they were a 'mixed bunch'; some were known to Gibson and transferred at his request, for example from 106 Squadron, his previous squadron. Others were moved as was convenient to the Group. In Melvin's case, his 'C' Flight of 57 Squadron was posted *in toto* across the station on 25 March. Possibly Charles Whitworth had recommended that Melvin should be considered for the new 'special squadron' that was forming on his base.

These 'C' Flight crews were led by Melvin, Flight Lieutenant William (Bill) Astell, Pilot Officer Geoff Rice and Flight Sergeant Ray Lovell. They had not volunteered for this unknown assignment. Rice protested but to no avail. Lovell was posted back to 57 Squadron after two weeks – *'the crew did not come up to the standards necessary for this squadron'*. Like Melvin, Astell had been a Wellington pilot in Egypt, with 148 Squadron; a twenty-three year old Mancunian, he had survived a crash-landing in the desert after being attacked by a German night fighter over Derna, started walking back and was picked up by a British Army advanced reconnaissance unit and returned to his squadron. Bill Astell was awarded the DFC in August 1942. At least there was a bonus for these ex-57 Squadron officers – they did not have to move from Scampton's substantial mess accommodation.

Given Melvin's experience of administration and training in the Middle East and the USA, it was natural that he should have been made one of the two flight commanders. He was to take much of the load from Gibson in organizing the heavy training programme which was necessary. Indeed, Gibson wrote afterwards that 'Melvyn [sic] had been responsible for a good deal of the training which made this raid possible. He had endeared himself to the boys.' Geoff Rice remarked of Melvin, 'He lived with a typewriter, a fantastic administrator' – again his experience of typing was coming in useful. Gibson also wrote that Melvin could down a pint of beer faster than anyone if he chose to do so.

The second flight commander was Squadron Leader H E Maudslay DFC who joined 617 on 25 March from 50 Squadron, along with Les Knight, an Australian Pilot Officer, and their crews. Henry Eric Maudslay, from Broadway, Worcestershire, was only twenty-one years old and had been both a middle distance runner and Captain of Boats at Eton. He was well liked, being remembered as 'a wonderful guy, a real gentleman' and 'quiet, kind, purposeful – nothing was too much trouble'.

Melvin and Henry Maudslay arranged the newly arrived crews into two flights. The general administration of the squadron was in the capable hands of the adjutant, Flight Lieutenant Harry R Humphries, who had transferred to Scampton from Gibson's former 106 Squadron base at Syerston. Humphries was to be

104 Squadron, Rolls-Royce Merlin Engined Wellington II, Egypt 1942. W/Cdr Philip Beare, centre, with Melvin Young on his right and S/Ldr Brown on his left.

Gibson's 'right hand man' on the ground. He recalled Melvin as being rather older and quieter than the rest of the squadron, and with a habit of sitting cross legged, sometimes on his desk, which some of his flight found a bit 'off-putting'.

In Melvin's 'A' Flight were the crews led by:

Flight Lieutenant Bill Astell DFC, born in Derbyshire in 1920, joined the RAFVR in 1939 and trained in UK and Africa.

Flight Lieutenant David Maltby DFC, born at Hastings in1920. He was training as a mining engineer pre-war. He joined the RAFVR in 1940 and trained in the UK before serving with 106 Squadron on Hampdens.

Flight Lieutenant David Shannon DFC, RAAF, born in South Australia in 1922. He joined the RAAF in 1941 and trained in Canada and then served under Guy Gibson in 106 Squadron, completing thirty-six operations.

Flight Lieutenant Robert Barlow DFC, RAAF, born in 1911 he joined the RAAF in 1941 and trained in Canada. He served with 61 Squadron on Lancasters at Syerston.

Pilot Officer Geoff Rice, born in 1917 at Portsmouth, but then lived at Hinckley, Leicestershire. He joined the RAF in 1941 and trained in the USA and Canada, arriving at 57 Squadron in December 1942.

Pilot Officer Warner Ottley DFC, born in 1923 in Battersea and grew up in Herne Bay. He joined the RAF

Flight Lieutenant David Shannon DFC, RAAF.

in 1941 and trained in UK and Canada, before serving with 83 and 207 Squadrons.

Pilot Officer William Divall (replacing Flight Sergeant Lovellon 10 April 1943) joined the RAFVR in 1941 and trained in Canada and progressed via OTUs and 1660 CU at Swinderby to join 57 Squadron at Scampton in February 1943. His was one of two 617 crews who were not able to take part in Operation *Chastise*.

Flight Sergeant Ken Brown, RCAF, born in 1920 at Moose Jaw, Canada. He joined the RCAF in 1941 and came to the UK in 1942, joining 44 Squadron in February 1943, shortly before his transfer to 617. He eventually transferred to 6 (RCAF) Group and remained in the RCAF until 1968.

Pilot Officer Vernon Byers, RCAF, born in Star City, Saskatchewan, Canada. He joined the RCAF in 1941 and trained in Manitoba before coming to the UK and joined 467 Squadron (RAAF) in February 1943, and then 617.

Thus Melvin's flight contained a representative selection of British and Commonwealth pilots, several decorated, and with a range of experience. Other aircrew members were not always as experienced. In the squadron as a whole, the average age was twenty-three, with a range of twenty to thirty-two, and by no means all had finished two tours; some had not done one. Nonetheless there was a good cadre of experience from

which Gibson could select pilots to attack the principal targets. It has been said that Bomber Command represented a microcosm of British society and 617 Squadron roughly met this description. The squadron and flight commanders were products of famous independent schools and, in Melvin's case, an American equivalent also, as well as Oxford. The other pilots were from a range of backgrounds but were mostly officers. The 'technical' aircrew members (flight engineers, wireless operators, gunners) generally were sergeants from various trades in civilian life. It was still an age when there was a distinct separation between officers and other ranks, and not just in the armed services. Attitudes of deference were in decline, accelerated by the war, but had some way still to fall by modern standards. The relationship between aircraft captains and aircrew members varied from crew to crew. One of Melvin's sergeant crew members observed that he expected to be called 'sir' even in flight – this would be consistent with his background, but may also be a reflection of his determination to form his inexperienced crew into a disciplined unit.

It is interesting to look in more detail at the six men he welded into an efficient crew for the Dams raid.

Sergeant David Taylor Horsfall, the flight engineer, was born in Leeds in 1920. In 1936 he joined the RAF as a boy entrant at the technical apprentice school at RAF Halton and served as a ground technician until 1942 when he graduated to aircrew status. His brother, Albert, had been killed in 1940 serving as a navigator in a Hampden with 50 Squadron.

Sergeant Charles Walpole Roberts, the navigator, was born in 1921 at Cromer in Norfolk. He was a trainee accountant before joining the RAF in 1940. He was sent to Rhodesia for flying training, where, after some time at Elementary Flying Training School, he was trained as a navigator. Many would-be pilots, if they did not quickly show flying ability, were moved on to navigating. Roberts' familiarity with figures would have been valuable in that role.

It is interesting to speculate whether Melvin would have been selected for further pilot training if he had joined after the start of the war, when large numbers of prospective pilots were being hurriedly screened for flying aptitude. Charles Whitworth's comment, 'He is not a natural pilot' on his OUAS report is pertinent – Melvin undoubtedly became an accomplished pilot, but this was the result of his determined application to the job rather than an inherent talent.

Sergeant Lawrence William Nichols, the wireless operator, was the oldest aircrew member in the squadron having been born at Northwood, Middlesex on 17 May

> 'Melvin undoubtedly became an accomplished pilot, but this was the result of his determined application to the job rather than an inherent talent.'

617 SQUADRON - SUMMER 1943

1910, and thus died before dawn on his thirty-third birthday. He was married to Georgina and had joined the RAF in 1940. He trained at the RAF Signals School at Yatesbury, where Melvin had received treatment for his leg in 1939, and Air Gunners' School at Pembrey in Wales – wireless operators had to double up as gunners on some aircraft types.

Flying Officer Vincent Sandford MacCausland, the bomb aimer, was born in 1913 in Prince Edward Island and in 1940 joined the Royal Canadian Air Force, in which his brother also served. Like most Canadian aircrew he was commissioned. His role as bomb aimer also required an aptitude for navigating, especially map reading at low level on Operation *Chastise*. Sergeant Wilfred Ibbotson, the rear gunner, was born in Wakefield in 1913. He was married to Doris, who lived at Bretton West in Yorkshire, and had joined the RAF in 1941. He trained at the No 4 Air Gunners' School at Morpeth, Northumberland and at No 10 OTU at Abingdon on Whitleys, and thus would have had this in common with Melvin.

Sergeant Gordon Alexander Yeo, the front gunner, was born at Barry, Glamorgan in 1922 and was the youngest of this older than average crew. He had joined the RAF in 1941 and was sent to No 32 Elementary Flying Training School in Alberta, Canada. He evidently did not succeed as a pilot and eventually attended the No 1 Air Armament School at Manby and became an air gunner. Thus Melvin's crew averaged over twenty-seven years of age, which was old for aircrew.

TRAINING

Initially the squadron was told to practise low level flying by day and night to achieve a high standard of navigation, mostly by clock, compass and map reading, for which the use of salient ground features was most important. Group Captain Satterly, the Senior Air Staff Officer at 5 Group, took advice on low level route finding from Group Captain E H 'Mouse' Fielden, MVO, AFC, who had flown many low level, special duties operations from Tempsford, Bedfordshire, where he was now Station Commander. Fielden later became an Air Commodore and was re-appointed to his pre-war position as Captain of the King's Flight. Fielden's note of 7 April 1943 recommended that pinpoints were best at water features such as bends in rivers or bridges over rivers. He advised that the coast was the most dangerous place; it should be crossed as low as possible, diving to gain speed. Ironically, he suggested a pinpoint at the lake at Akersloot in Holland on the homeward route, then west to the coast – this is the place where Melvin was to be shot down!

A series of cross-country routes were devised and many of these involved flying over lakes in the Midlands and Wales. In particular, Bala Lake in Wales, the

> 'The crews did not know that they were to attack dams until the pre-flight briefing on the day of the attack – indeed Melvin and Henry Maudslay were not told until the day before.'

Derwent reservoir near Sheffield, the Abberton reservoir near Colchester and the Eyebrook reservoir near Corby were used. The last of these, Eyebrook, also referred to as Uppingham Lake, had been built to provide water for the nearby British steelworks! The crews did not know that they were to attack dams until the pre-flight briefing on the day of the attack – indeed Melvin and Henry Maudslay were not told until the day before – but they soon found themselves aiming at targets, on the Wainfleet bombing range (in the Wash) and at Eyebrook, which were set up to simulate the two towers on the Möhne Dam. The bomb aimers were provided with a hand-held ranging sight to tell them when to release the weapon; this used the known distance between the towers and simple trigonometry. However, some bomb aimers found this difficult to hold steady and improvised other means of measuring the dropping point. The Eyebrook reservoir was also much used to practise using the two spot-lights to get the correct height above the surface, although sometimes they were tried over the aerodrome and the waters of the Wash.

The Type 464 Lancasters were not immediately available when the squadron formed, so they were equipped with ten standard aircraft, borrowed from other squadrons, for initial training. These were pressed into service without delay. Bill Astell was sent off, on 27 March, to photograph many lakes and reservoirs all over Britain, 'on the pretext that they might be needed for training crews at Conversion Units'. The next day Gibson took a Lancaster with Melvin and John Hopgood to assess their ability to fly low over water. Hopgood was one of the 'B' Flight pilots who had been with Gibson in 106 Squadron and in whom he had especial confidence, as he had helped Gibson to convert to the Lancaster. They used the Derwent reservoir and found the task very dangerous as dusk fell. This led to the requirement for a system to measure the height accurately – advice was taken from Farnborough where a civilian scientist, Benjamin Lockspeiser, suggested the spotlight solution.

From early in April Melvin and his crew started flying in earnest. There were many bombing runs, using small practice bombs, at the Wainfleet range and cross-country exercises around the country. On 5 April, in standard Lancaster W4921, Melvin and his crew did a five hour flight routing Stafford, Lake Vyrnwy, Caldey Island (Pembrokeshire), Wells (Somerset), Hunstanton (Norfolk), Wainfleet and back to Scampton. Gordon Yeo, who came from Barry in South Wales, wrote to his parents:

> *'We have just come back from a trip of five hours. We were flying quite close to Barry this morning. We flew right down the coast and came back round Cornwall and Bridgewater – a*

lovely trip. We were flying in our shirt sleeves half the time as it was so hot.'

There were also various technical flights, such as air tests after maintenance, to be performed. One day Melvin took an aircraft (ED763) to Waddington, just on the other side of Lincoln, to be fitted with 'Two Stage Amber', a blue transparency fitted to the perspex in two of the Lancasters, to be used in conjunction with yellow goggles to simulate moonlight conditions in daytime. Throughout April Melvin managed to fly some thirty-seven hours, but thirty-two of these were in daytime. No doubt his administrative duties interfered, but he must have been eager to get back into flying practice after so long away from operations. By the time of the raid he had accumulated only sixty hours since the squadron was formed, of which twenty-one were at night. On 22 April, Lancaster Type 464, ED887/G (the G showed it must be guarded) was taken on charge by 617 Squadron with the squadron identification AJ-A; this was to be Melvin's aircraft for most of his subsequent flying and the raid. AJ was the two letter aircraft identification code assigned to 617 Squadron; each aircraft had its own additional separate letter, in Melvin's case 'A for Apple'.

On 1 May Melvin flew – at low level (200 feet) – with Gibson, Whitworth and some of the more experienced members of the squadron to Manston, which is near the eastern corner of Kent and the shallow water at Reculver where trial drops of Upkeep were to take place. These test flights were mostly with inert weapons filled with concrete, although at least one live example was tested. The next two weeks saw Melvin and his crew flying more at night, with numerous 'spotlight runs' and cross-country flights.

Early in May Gibson had reported that he felt his crews would be able to perform the operation, albeit practice continued at an intense pace. Melvin flew a variety of cross-country and bombing exercises, visiting the lakes at Uppingham, Colchester, Sheffield (Derwent) and the range at Wainfleet. On one flight he had Bill Astell with him and on another Warner Ottley – both

Melvin and his crew in a dinghy, 8 October 1940. He made two ditchings in the sea this year and had to be rescued.

were to die on the way to the dams.

On 9 May Melvin and Henry Maudslay flew their aircraft in company to test newly fitted Very High Frequency radio telephone (R/T) sets. These VHF sets had been installed to enable adequate voice communication between aircraft captains in order to control the attack on the dams. Radio silence would be maintained as far as possible and essential communications with 5 Group HQ would be by Wireless/Telegraphy (W/T), the wireless operators sending and receiving messages in Morse code. However it soon became clear that tactical control around the dams would need voice control, thus the fitting of these VHF sets, previously only installed in fighter aircraft.

The Chief Signals Officer at 5 Group HQ in 1943, Wing Commander W E Dunn, had been the signals officer for 102 Squadron when Melvin made his two ditchings in the sea in 1940. For Operation *Chastise*, Dunn had devised a system of code words for

Navigating and flying a Lancaster for six hours, at very low altitude, at night, over enemy territory, was both physically and mentally exhausting.

A photograph showing the huge splash created by the first bounce of the bomb. The powerful plume of water damaged the Lancaster which was flown by Henry Maudslay during the raid.

communication to and from the aircraft. The most significant of these were 'Nigger', to be sent when the Möhne Dam had been breached, and 'Dinghy' (Melvin's nickname), when the Eder had been broken. Nigger was the name of Gibson's black Labrador dog, which was to be tragically killed on the day before the raid.

On 11 May Melvin flew 'Cross country route number 1, returning direct from Colchester' in formation with the aircraft of Maltby and Shannon, with whom he would be flying en route to the dams. From 11 to 13 May various aircraft from 617 flew to Reculver and dropped inert Upkeep weapons towards the beach. It is not recorded whether Melvin was one of these, but as one of the crews chosen to take part in the attack on the principal target, the Möhne Dam, it is likely that he did. Certainly the other flight commander, Henry Maudslay, dropped one on 13 May and the splash from the first bounce damaged his aircraft so badly that it could not be repaired in time for the raid.

Later that day (13 May) a 'dress rehearsal operation' was flown via the lakes at Uppingham and Colchester, which Gibson noted as 'Completely successful'. Section Officer Fay Gillan, one of the intelligence officers at Scampton, flew on this exercise with Flight Lieutenant Harold 'Mick' Martin, an Australian with operational experience on Hampdens and Lancasters and a noted expert in low flying; she found it a most memorable and exciting experience. All was set for Operation *Chastise*.

THE RAID

On 15 May the Executive Order for Operation *Chastise* was issued – the raid was to be flown the next night, 16/17 May. The weather forecast was good and the moon (which was full in the period 17-20 May) would rise at 17.00 and set at 04.31 (all times in British Double Summer Time, GMT plus two hours). During the afternoon of 15 May, Barnes Wallis was flown to Scampton, in a Wellington of course, and Melvin was called to a meeting at the Station Commander's house. At this meeting, Melvin, Henry Maudslay, John Hopgood, who had been selected to be deputy leader for the attack on the Möhne Dam, and Flight Lieutenant

Bob Hay, the Australian who was the squadron's bombing leader, were briefed by Wallis and Gibson on the targets, the details of the weapon and its delivery. Such was the level of security that the rest of the aircrews were not told until the pre-raid briefing on 16 May, when models of the Möhne and Sorpe dams were available for inspection, as well as photographs of the other targets. This full briefing, principally by Wallis and Gibson, was very thorough and caused considerable excitement,and possibly some relief that it was not to be the battleship *Tirpitz*. Eighteen months later that ominous ship was sunk by 617 Squadron using a different bomb, also designed by Wallis.

The plan for the operation was that three waves of aircraft would be employed. The first wave of nine aircraft, led by Gibson, would attack the Möhne Dam, then the Eder, followed by other targets as directed by wireless from 5 Group HQ if any weapons were still available. This wave would fly in three sections of three aircraft, about ten minutes apart, led by Guy Gibson, Melvin Young and Henry Maudslay. Melvin was to fly accompanied by David Maltby and David Shannon. The second wave would fly, by a different route to confuse enemy defences, to the Sorpe Dam. Indeed, because this route was slightly longer via the islands off north Holland, the second wave actually took off before the first wave. The third wave, also of five aircraft, was to set off later and act as a mobile reserve to be used against such dams as were still unbroken. In all, nineteen Type 464 aircraft and their crews were available. The crews of Divall and Wilson had sickness and one aircraft could not be repaired from damage during training.

The Operational Executive Order required that the raid be flown at low level, not above 500 feet, except between Ahlen, the final waypoint, and the target – where the leader of each section should climb to 1,000 feet ten miles from the target, presumably to ensure finding the target with certainty. For reasons of surprise, it would be desirable to fly as low as possible to reduce the chance of being seen by the German radar, and thus risk interception by fighters, and to minimize the time of exposure to anti-aircraft guns (flak). The 500 feet limit was an acceptance that it would be essential to identify turning points accurately and the section leaders would have felt a particular responsibility to ensure that they kept to the route, which had been devised to avoid known flak locations as far as possible. After the raid Maltby and Shannon commented that Melvin had shown a tendency to fly higher than them, and they had used Aldis signal lamps to warn him to keep low. For his part he would have been feeling a great responsibility to lead his team accurately. It may also be that, with relatively little recent flying, on his first operation in a Lancaster and his first at all for nearly a year, and with a crew with little operational experience, he was more

A German Anti-Aircraft team scan the sky for enemy aircraft.

concerned about hitting obstacles on the ground than they were – he had never seen himself as 'the fighter pilot type'!

The hazards of low level operations over enemy territory were such that Harris generally disapproved of using heavy bombers in this role. Operation *Chastise* was an exception, but the loss on the raid of several aircraft to flak and surface impact supports Harris's general view. It was easy to stray off the route – indeed Gibson missed his turning point at the River Rhine by several miles and had an uncomfortable few minutes getting back on track, being shot at in doing so. One of the second wave aircraft, flown by Geoff Rice, got so low over water in Holland that its Upkeep weapon was torn from the aircraft, albeit Rice got the aircraft home. It should be emphasized that to navigate and fly a Lancaster, which had no power assistance to the controls, for six hours, at very low altitude, at night, over enemy territory, was both physically and mentally exhausting.

So, after the main briefing, the navigators and bomb aimers, who had a vital map reading role at low level, set about marking their maps and preparing their navigation logs, while other crew members relaxed as best they could. Melvin, characteristically, tidied his office. In due course the aircrew had a pre-operational meal. Such was the security that it was only when they were served with bacon and eggs, a delight reserved in wartime for aircrew on operations, that sharp observers such as Fay Gillan deduced that this was for real; no more a practice. No doubt there was the usual fatalistic humour in the vein 'If you don't come back, can I have your next egg'. Thence to get kitted up and go out to the waiting aircraft around the perimeter of the airfield, which was still a large grass aerodrome at this time; it was due to be laid with hard runways shortly after the Dams Raid.

At 2128 the first of the second wave aircraft, AJ-E flown by Flight Lieutenant Barlow, took off, followed in quick succession by Munro (AJ-W), Byers (AJ-K) and Rice (AJ-H). None of these reached their target, the Sorpe Dam. Barlow and Byers were shot down or

'Over the Wash they let down even lower and tested the spotlights on the water, calibrating the aircraft's pressure altimeters in the process.'

crashed en route, Munro was hit by flak and had to return and, as mentioned before, Geoff Rice had a close call when his aircraft hit the surface and lost its weapon. Flight Lieutenant McCarthy DFC RCAF, a very determined American, was delayed by technical trouble before take-off, transferred to a spare aircraft (AJ-T) and took off half an hour later – he did reach the Sorpe and made a skilful and persistent attack, but only achieved relatively minor damage.

At 2139 Guy Gibson (AJ-G) took off followed by Hopgood (AJ-M) and Martin (AJ-P). They formed up in close formation and came back overhead to set course. At 2147 Melvin lined A for Apple up for take-off, David Horsfall applied full power (3,000 rpm +14 lbs/sq in boost) and they rumbled and bounced across the grass field until flying speed was attained and Melvin could ease the heavy aircraft off the ground, retract the main wheels and concentrate on getting the airspeed up and the climb safely established. Maltby (AJ-J) and Shannon (AJ-L) and their crews were soon off the ground in turn and the three aircraft formed up and set course overhead Scampton at 2158.

THE FLIGHT TO THE MÖHNE DAM

It is fortunate that the navigation log of Sergeant V Nicholson, in David Maltby's AJ-J, has survived and so the progress of Melvin's section of three aircraft is well described. The first note in the log on getting airborne was that the IFF (Identify Friend or Foe) radio was switched on, to ensure that British radar knew they were indeed 'one of ours'. Within a few minutes they had settled at a height of 150 feet and were over Woodhall Spa and shortly after were crossing the north-west coast of the Wash about five miles north-east of Boston. Perhaps they could see the Boston Stump, the tallest parish church tower in Britain, silhouetted against the evening sky, the sun having just set. Over the Wash they let down even lower and tested the spotlights on the water, calibrating the aircraft's pressure altimeters in the process. Soon the south-east coast of the Wash flashed by and they were over Norfolk, not far from the Royal Family's country house at Sandringham. Their route took them via East Dereham (near the USAAF base at Shipdham where Melvin had landed the previous month), Wymondham, Bungay on the River Waveney in Suffolk and on to Southwold with its distinctive lighthouse, where they crossed the English coast at 2238, having made a ground speed of 175 mph from Scampton with a slight northerly wind helping them along. Blacked-out Southwold in the twilight was to be the last sight of Britain for Melvin and his crew.

This was a good point for the navigators to take stock of their calculations of the wind, not very strong fortunately, and to restart plotting the aircraft's position from a known point. They were then over the North Sea, with only a very small change of track to their next way point at the mouth of the River Scheldt in Holland, between the islands of Schouwen and Walcheren. The IFF could now be switched off – no unnecessary radio transmissions to give away their position to a vigilant enemy. According to Nicholson's log the three aircraft maintained the same average speed (175 mph, ninety-nine miles in thirty-five minutes) and arrived at the Scheldt waypoint at 2312, on track. As if to demonstrate the difficulty of such navigation, Gibson's section had drifted somewhat south and crossed the heavily defended Walcheren, fortunately without mishap. At this point the bomb aimers armed the self destructive fuses in the Upkeep weapons.

Now began the difficult task of flying low over enemy territory and finding the way while avoiding obstacles such as power lines and pylons – both the front gunner and the bomb aimer had a literally vital role in looking out for such hazards and warning the pilot to pull up in good time. The route had been chosen with easily identifiable way-points and reasonably short distances between them, avoiding known flak concentrations as far as possible. As they flew in over the eastern arm of the Scheldt there were good coast-line features to confirm that they were on track to the next waypoint at the small town of Roosendaal, which is a short distance inland from the estuary and distinguished by a railway junction. They had to take some evasive action from flak on this leg of the route, and the ground speed declined to 162 mph, perhaps due to a combination of this manoeuvring and an increasing easterly component in the wind.

Having passed Roosendaal at 2325 the route required a small heading change to the left to pass south of Breda and Tilburg and pick up the helpful line feature of the Wilhelmina Canal. This feature would guide them clear of the heavily defended aerodromes at Gilze-Rijen (between Breda and Tilburg) on their left and Eindhoven on the right. It was vitally important to avoid these airfields as was to be shown, tragically, later that night when one of the third wave aircraft, AJ-S, flown by Pilot Officer Lewis Burpee DFM, RCAF, strayed over Gilze-Rijen and was brought down by the defences.

Eindhoven was the location of the important Philips radio factory which had been pressed into service for the Germans and had been the target for the daring low-level daylight raid, Operation *Oyster*, by the medium bombers – Bostons and Mosquitos – of 2 Group on 6 December 1942. This raid had achieved much damage but at a cost of twelve of the seventy-eight attacking aircraft. The defences had been strong then and could be expected to be even more dangerous five months on.

'Gibson's section had drifted somewhat south and crossed the heavily defended Walcheren, fortunately without mishap. At this point the bomb aimers armed the self-destructive fuses in the Upkeep weapons.'

Beyond Eindhoven the canal met another, at right angles, by a village called Beek and this made a prominent waypoint. Melvin's section arrived at Beek at 2342 and Nicholson observed that 'Leader turned soon' – perhaps Melvin was a bit higher than the others to be sure of seeing the turning point and anticipated the turn, of some 20 degrees left, towards the next waypoint at Rees on the River Rhine which they reached at 2356.

Melvin's section was now averaging about 170 mph ground speed. Nicholson recorded that the electronic navigational aid GEE was 'jammed something chronic' at this time. GEE was a 'hyperbolic' area navigation system, similar to the later Decca and LORAN systems, which sent signals from three transmitters in England. These signals could be plotted by the navigators on special charts to give a reasonably accurate fix of position. However, like all such radio aids the enemy could be relied on to try to interfere with the signals. Most of the navigators on the raid had trouble with GEE, except Knight's navigator, Hobday; perhaps he was particularly adept at operating the quite complex receiver.

From Rees they flew almost due east to a group of lakes near Dulmen. On this leg they met some well-directed flak which again caused them to take evasive action. Although Melvin and his section got through this area successfully, Henry Maudslay's group was less fortunate. Bill Astell's aircraft (AJ-B) fell some way behind the others and shortly afterwards, at 0015, hit a power pylon and crashed near Marbeck, three miles south of Borken. The Upkeep broke away from the rest of the wreckage and careered on across the fields before its self-destruct fuse set it off, making a large crater. This event is prominent in the folk memory of the area and is commemorated in a small museum in a nearby village. Astell, who had survived the desert war by skill and courage, had now run out of luck. Another member of Melvin's 'A' Flight, Robert Barlow in AJ-E, had already crashed just east of Rees having hit high tension wires. Barlow's weapon did not explode and was recovered and analysed by the Germans. Barlow was the first of the second wave which had followed a more northerly route before turning at Rees. This aircraft crashed at 2350, just minutes before Melvin passed nearby. The hazards of low flying were starting to take their toll.

Having reached the Dulmen waypoint at 0009 they turned 15 degrees right to head for Ahlen which had a conspicuous railway line. Ahlen was successfully identified at 0020 and they turned right again onto a south-south-easterly heading to pass between the small towns of Werl and Soest, having to take more evasive action. Coming now into somewhat more hilly country and approaching the Möhne, Melvin would have climbed AJ-A to make sure he could see the lake in good time. It was now 0026, although Shannon arrived slightly after the other two and was shot at by the defences for his trouble. Nicholson's log records that they now switched on their VHF radio sets and started circling in pre-arranged locations, and commented that the 'flak [was] none too light'. They had arrived at the principal target. In Gibson's words:

'As we came over the hill, we saw the Möhne Lake. Then we saw the dam itself. In that light it looked squat and heavy and unconquerable; it looked grey and solid in the moonlight as though it were part of the countryside itself and just as immovable.'

THE ATTACK ON THE MÖHNE DAM

The scene was now set for the most famous and ingenious attack in the history of the RAF – requiring a degree of precision not to be repeated until the advent of sophisticated electronic guidance systems. It was conducted with remarkable skill and great courage.

The Möhne lake (Möhnesee) is aligned east-west and has two main arms separated by a wooded peninsula on which the highest point is called the Heversberg. The larger, northern arm is fed by the Möhne River and is crossed by two road bridges at the villages of Delecke and Korbecke. The shorter, southern arm (Hevearm des

Möhnesees on the map) is fed by a small river, the Heve. The dam, which is some 650 metres long, 30 metres high and 30 metres thick at the base, lies at the north-west corner of the lake. It is aligned roughly north-east to south-west, and to attack it at right angles to its centre point required the aircraft to fly in on a heading of approximately 330 degrees (30 degrees west of north). The Heversberg rises to 262 metres (860 feet) above sea level and the lake surface, when full, is at 214 metres (700 feet). The dam was defended by a dozen quick firing anti-aircraft guns, some on the towers of the dam and some in the surrounding country. Just below the air face of the dam was a hydroelectric power station.

The geography of the dam and the performance of the aircraft made it necessary to attack by lining up over the Hevearm, diving and skimming down the Heversburg peninsula, just above the trees, to gain the necessary speed (220mph) to release the weapon. Indeed Gibson's account tells us that his bomb aimer warned him: 'You're going to hit those trees.' However it was indeed necessary to get down to the bombing height as early as possible in the run – the author's calculations show that if the aircraft was levelled off 1,650 yards from the dam (the shore is only 1,900 yards out), then at 220mph there would be only eleven seconds before reaching the release

MÖHNE LAKE AND DAM LINE OF ATTACK

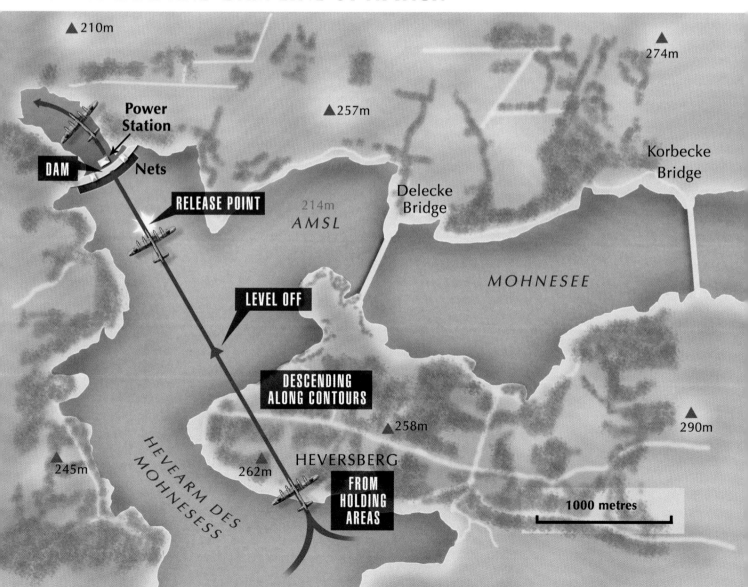

point at 450 yards; not much time, but just enough for a well-trained, determined crew. In this short time the height had to be settled at 60 feet and the line adjusted to aim at the centre of the dam, with the wings level. A firm grip on the control wheel would have been needed even if the adrenalin was not pumping – Melvin's rowing muscles would now be a bonus.

The engine throttles would have been adjusted by the flight engineer to maintain the speed gained in the dive. In addition to the noise and vibration from the engines and propellers, high enough anyway, there would have been the added vibration, with a different frequency and amplitude, of the weapon rotating at 500 rpm – as it needed to be run up ten minutes before the attack. Although the weapons were balanced as well as possible, it was reported that they did cause a noticeable vibration.

Some books on the raid have shown the line of attack as being along the northern arm of the lake, followed by a right turn, which would have to be through at least seventy degrees, to line up towards the dam. The author's calculations have shown that this would have required a bank angle of approximately fifty degrees, more or less depending on assumptions, which, with a Lancaster wingspan of 102 feet, would result in the wing tip being only twenty feet above the water. Experienced pilots are unlikely to have contemplated this sort of semi-aerobatic manoeuvre in the dark – the merest sideslip would have put the wing in the water. After the turn there would only be about three to five seconds left to get the all important height, line and level attitude. Also the associated load factor ('g' loading) in the turn would be over 1.5g and this would result in a loss of speed. Inspection of the briefing model for the Möhne, on display at the Imperial War Museum, confirms, in the author's opinion, that the only practical option would have been to descend straight over the Heversberg.

On arrival at the Möhne, Gibson circled the lake and dam to 'size it up' and said over the radio that 'he liked the look of it'. At this time, 0026, Young's section arrived. The tactic was that Gibson would attack first with the others orbiting at low altitude in agreed positions nearby. They would come in to attack in turn at the leader's command – he would call them on VHF using the call-sign 'Cooler', with a number denoting their position in the order of action – thus AJ-A would be 'Cooler 4'. Gibson reminded Hopgood to take over from him should he be knocked out of the action. At 0028 Guy Gibson made the first attack in the face of significant anti-aircraft fire. His weapon bounced three times, sank and exploded sending up a column of water to about 1,000 feet. When the lake settled it could be seen that the dam was unbroken. A coded signal was sent by Gibson's wireless operator to 5 Group HQ, where Harris, Cochrane and Wallis were waiting expectantly, reporting that the 'mine' had exploded without breaching the dam. Subsequent analysis supports this report: the weapon may have stopped and sunk just short of the dam, possibly having hit and broken the anti-torpedo nets thus clearing the way for following weapons.

Next, Hopgood was called in to attack, just as Maudslay and Knight arrived at 0032. It seems likely that Hopgood's aircraft had been hit by flak on the flight to the Möhne and that Hopgood himself had been injured. Undeterred, he made his run at the dam but was hit again and his aircraft fatally damaged, catching fire and eventually exploding. Thus it seems, not surprisingly, that the crew had difficulty getting all the necessary conditions right for the release. However the bomb aimer, realizing the aircraft was doomed, released the weapon anyway, too late, and it bounced over the dam and fell on the power station below. It was destroyed in a blinding flash when the delayed action fuse detonated the high explosive, at about the time that the aircraft crashed some six kilometres from the dam where it burned fiercely throughout the rest of the action. With notable heroism, which received no official recognition later, Hopgood climbed the aircraft as high as he could, and said to his crew, 'For Christ's sake get out'. Two of them, the bomb aimer Flight Sergeant J W Fraser, RCAF and the rear gunner Pilot Officer A F Burcher, DFM, RAAF, did manage to escape despite the low altitude. Flight Lieutenant John Vere Hopgood, from Seaford in Sussex, already held the DFC and Bar and was only twenty-one years old. He had prophesied to Shannon just before take-off: 'I think this is going to be a tough one, and I don't think I'm coming back, Dave.'

Next it was the turn of Flight Lieutenant Harold B 'Mick' Martin DFC, an Australian who had joined the RAF. At 0038 he made his run. This time Gibson flew in somewhat ahead and to the right of Martin, to distract the German defences, and let his own gunners engage them. Both aircraft survived the flak, although Martin's aircraft was hit but not badly damaged. Martin's bomb aimer was Flight Lieutenant R C 'Bob' Hay, DFC, RAAF whose experience had led to his being made the squadron bombing leader. A huge explosion and column of water resulted from this weapon, such that the rear gunner could not see how many bounces had been achieved. Unfortunately this weapon had veered off to the left and exploded near the southern shore of the lake. The defenders were shaken and drenched but the dam was still there. The most likely explanation was that the Upkeep had met the water slightly off level and thus did not bounce straight. Wallis was aware that the cylindrical design was vulnerable to this effect, but had been forced to adopt this design after unsuccessful experiments with a spherical shape.

Then at 0043 Melvin and his crew made their attempt. Melvin would have climbed AJ-A from its holding orbit to a height which practice had told him would be enough to achieve 220mph after a shallow dive, with the weapon on. He visually lined up with the centre of the dam and pushed the nose down to gain speed, following the contours of the Heversberg peninsula as closely as he dared. He may have trimmed the elevator to ease some of his forward push on the control wheel, but would probably have left some nose-up trim in case he needed to go around or was himself hit, in which case the aircraft would climb and give the crew some chance of survival. Meanwhile Larry Nichols, the wireless operator, had checked that the weapon was rotating at 500 rpm – it would probably have been set running soon after they reached the Möhne. Charles Roberts, the navigator, had switched on the spotlights and positioned himself by the starboard blister in the cockpit canopy in order to give Melvin up/down guidance over the water surface. David Horsfall, the flight engineer, controlled the engine throttles and kept a close watch on the airspeed indicator, aiming to have the speed at 220 mph as they levelled over the lake and pushed the levers forward as necessary to maintain that speed. The airgunners, Gordon Yeo and Wilfred Ibbotson, prepared to engage the defences – all the squadron guns were loaded with tracer ammunition the better to assess their aim and, hopefully, frighten the enemy.

Gibson, whose leadership throughout can only be described as heroic, was now flying on the air side of the dam to distract the enemy gunners and Martin flew in alongside AJ-A to draw some of the flak. We can only conjecture what it was like for Melvin as they rushed down over the trees and he levelled off quickly as near to 60 feet as he could judge, listening for Roberts' voice to guide him up or down, and for Vincent MacCausland, lying in the bomb aimer's position, calling, if necessary, for slight adjustments in heading, which needed to be made with firm but smooth pressure on the rudders, with a bit of aileron to ensure that the wings stayed level. Meanwhile Gordon Yeo was shooting at the guns on the dam, some of which would have been returning his fire. Larry Nichols was prepared to fire a red Very flare when they had dropped the weapon and crossed the dam. The moon was behind the aircraft, thus silhouetting them for the flak gunners. And all this happened very fast – only about ten seconds from levelling off over the water until Vincent MacCausland pressed the release and their Upkeep fell away and started its career towards the dam.

After its release the weapon fell further behind the aircraft with each bounce and the rear gunner could see the plumes of spray. Gibson recorded that Young's weapon made 'three good bounces and contact' [with the dam]. It sank to its preset depth and exploded against the dam wall as Wallis had predicted. Another huge column of water rose and a shock wave could be seen rippling through the lake. Melvin glanced back and thought he must have broken it – in fact later analysis indicated that the dam was now beginning to break but it did not collapse immediately. And so Nichols sent a wireless signal to HQ saying they had hit the dam but it was unbroken; the mood at 5 Group HQ was becoming despondent.

It was now David Maltby's turn to attack in AJ-J at 0049. Gibson and Martin orbited on the water side of the dam, engaging the flak positions, some of which had now been silenced, to take the heat off AJ-J. As Maltby raced in he saw that 'the crown of the wall was already crumbling ...a tremendous amount of debris on the

top...a breach in the centre of the dam'. With admirable presence of mind in the time available he adjusted his line slightly left and his weapon was released. It bounced four times, struck the dam, sank and exploded. In the initial confusion of flak and water it was not immediately obvious that the dam was now broken and Gibson called Shannon to get ready, but was soon able to tell him to hold off. When the spray had subsided Gibson was able to see that a great gap, some 150 metres long, had appeared in the dam and a torrent of water surged down the valley below – 'looking like stirred porridge in the moonlight'. There followed a lot of excited calls on the R/T – Maltby's navigator, Nicholson, recorded 'Bomb Dropped. Wizard' in his log. Thus about forty minutes after Gibson had reached the Möhne, the code word 'Nigger' was transmitted by Gibson's wireless operator, at 0056. This was received and decoded by Wing Commander Dunn at 5 Group HQ and the excitement there equalled that over the Möhne. Wallis danced for joy and Harris was delighted to find his scepticism had been misplaced.

ON TO THE EDER

There were now only three aircraft of the first wave armed with Upkeep; AJ-Z (Maudslay), AJ-L (Shannon) and AJ-N (Knight). Gibson called Astell, but to no avail; unknown to the others he and his crew had died just before Gibson had arrived at the Möhne. Conscious of the time, Gibson sent Martin and Maltby home and, with Melvin as his deputy, led the three armed aircraft towards the Eder Dam. This was a flight of about fifteen minutes over increasingly hilly country, with the pilots trying to keep down in the valleys as much as possible. Now well past midnight some mist was beginning to form under the clear skies. The Eder see (Ederstausee on some maps) is a very long lake with more than one arm and Shannon, at least, found it difficult to find the dam, until Gibson fired a Very light over it.

The Eder Dam was not defended by guns, but it was in very difficult terrain. It soon became clear that the only way to get down to the lake was by descending along a valley from beside the Schloss (Castle) at Waldeck, about two miles north of the dam on the other side of the lake. The descent from the castle was not directly towards the dam and there was another spur of land, shown on some maps as the Hammerberg, protruding into the lake on the ideal line towards the centre of the dam. It is not clear just what tactics each pilot chose to approach it. Probably a descending turn towards the dam was started as soon as they were clear of the valley, onto the best line they could make. There would then be very little time to get down and stabilized at 60 feet and 220 mph. Even then a line aimed at right angles to the centre of the dam was not feasible, possibly 25 degrees off, and this explains why the breach, when it was finally achieved, was towards the southern end of the dam.

It was going to take the three attacking aircraft eleven attempts to launch three weapons. To add insult to injury, on passing over the dam there is a significant mountain, the Michelskopf, directly ahead, requiring a climbing turn to avoid it. This would have been especially daunting when overshooting with the weapon still onboard – no doubt the Merlin engines were called on for emergency power, 'through the gate'. Melvin's role at the Eder was a watching brief, ready to take over from Gibson if necessary; if, for instance, Gibson had technical trouble with the VHF radio. Arguably this was the worst job of the night – very tense, hoping they would succeed and allow everyone to be on the way home before the dawn. Gibson ordered Shannon to make the first attack. It is best described in Dave Shannon's own words:

'The Eder was a bugger of a job....I was first to go; I tried three times to get a 'spot on' approach but was never satisfied. To get out of the valley after crossing the dam wall we had to put on full throttle and do a steep climbing turn to avoid a vast rock face. My exit with a 9000lb bomb revolving at 500rpm was bloody hairy. Then Gibson told us to take a breather and Henry Maudslay went in.'

Henry Maudslay and his crew made two runs without feeling able to release their weapon. Then Shannon tried again and after two more unsuccessful attempts launched his Upkeep at 0139. It bounced twice, hit the

> 'We saw the tremendous earthquake which shook the base of the dam, and then, as if a gigantic hand had punched a hole through cardboard, the whole thing collapsed.'

water face of the dam and sank, followed by the now expected explosion sending a column of water up to a great height. The dam did not immediately fall, but it was no doubt weakened. Then Henry Maudslay made another attempt and this time released the weapon, but just too late – it hit the parapet of the dam at high velocity and this impact caused the bomb to detonate spontaneously. Fortunately the aircraft had already passed the dam but, no doubt, felt the blast. Maudslay, asked on the radio if he was alright, was heard to reply, faintly 'I think so'. The others did not see him again. He seems to have struggled with a probably damaged aircraft and attempted to get home, only to be shot down near the German-Dutch border.

Now only Les Knight in AJ-N had a weapon. He made two attempts and on the second got into a good position and released the Upkeep at 0152. It bounced three times and hit the dam to the right of centre. Gibson described this attack:

'..we were flying above him, and about 400 yards to the right, and saw his mine hit the water. We saw where it sank. We saw the tremendous earthquake which shook the base of the dam, and then, as if a gigantic hand had punched a hole through cardboard, the whole thing collapsed.'

No doubt with great relief, Melvin's nick-name

THE ROUTE OF AJ-A

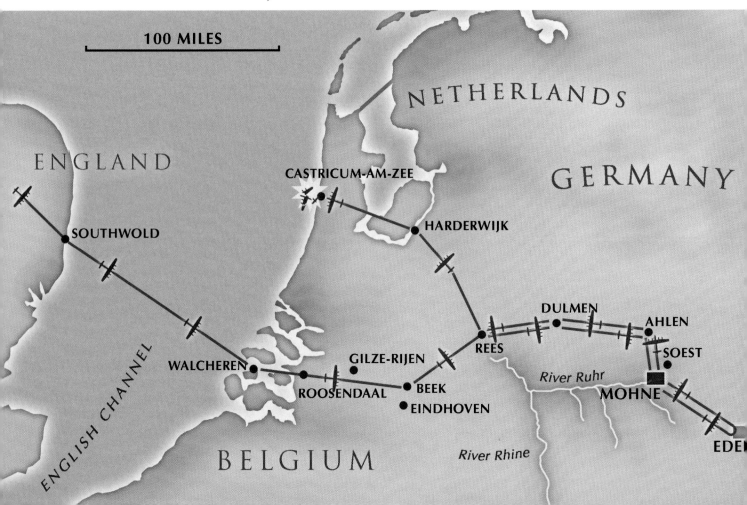

German photograph of Lancaster wreckage on the Dutch beach, thought to be AJ-A.

good chance of destroying an aircraft, and so it was. Whatever the reason, their luck had deserted them at the last hurdle and thus ended their historic and heroic last night.

At 0258 gunners at Castricum-aan-Zee reported shooting down an aircraft they took to be a Halifax, but it almost certainly was Melvin's Lancaster and several batteries also reported firing at it. AJ-A crashed into the sea and all its crew were killed. Over the North Sea, Guy Gibson called Melvin on the radio...there was no reply.

The surviving eleven Type 464 Provisioning Lancasters from Operation *Chastise* landed back at Scampton between 0311 and 0615 to be greeted and congratulated by Harris, Wallis and many others. Eight aircraft had been lost and fifty-three flyers had died. Much damage had been done to the enemy and the Royal Air Force's fame was enhanced forever.

'Dinghy' was transmitted back to 5 Group HQ, to be received with yet more celebration. Over the Eder it was time to get home.

While all this was going on at the Möhne and the Eder Dams, it should not be forgotten that other 617 Squadron pilots were making heroic attempts elsewhere. McCarthy and Brown made valiant attacks on the Sorpe, albeit frustrated by the unsuitability of Upkeep for that type of dam. Townsend launched a weapon unsuccessfully at another dam, late in the night, and had to race the dawn home crossing Holland in daylight.

FLIGHT BACK TO DISASTER

The four aircraft over the Eder now had a strong incentive to get home safely and as quickly as possible. Three return routes had been specified in the operational order; all involved retracing the route via the Möhne Dam, Ahlen and the lakes at Dulmen. From Dulmen there was some choice, but all routes involved crossing the Ijsselmeer (Zuider Zee) and the Helder peninsula in north Holland. Melvin and Guy Gibson seem to have chosen the most southerly route which continued back to the same crossing point on the Rhine at Rees, then north-west to near Harderwijkon the Ijsselmeer, across that stretch of water via the picturesque island village of Marken and on to leave the Dutch North Seacoast at a known 'gap' in the defences near Egmond. If, as seems likely, they set course from the Eder at approximately 0155, and given that Melvin in AJ-A seems to have reached the North Sea in a few minutes over one hour, he must have averaged a speed of about 215 mph – full throttle all the way and as low as possible.

It will never be known whether Melvin crossed the coast too high, or too near Ijmuiden – his inexperienced navigator, Charles Roberts, aided by Vincent MacCausland map reading in the nose of the aircraft, seems to have done an admirable job of helping the captain find the way previously. Melvin had demonstrated at the Möhne Dam that he had become a very accomplished pilot, and had trained his crew well. Nonetheless, one hit from a high explosive shell had a

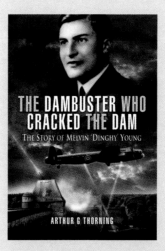

DAMBUSTER CRASH SITES AND THE MEN WHO DIDN'T COME HOME

By Chris Ward & Andreas Wachtel

This article was extracted from *Dambuster Crash Sites - 617 Dambuster Squadron Crash Sites in Holland & Germany* and is reproduced here by permission of Pen and Sword Books Ltd.

F/L J V HOPGOOD

ED925, AJ-MOSTÖNNEN, NORTH-WEST OF THE MÖHNESEE

At the time of his death John Hopgood was a mere twenty-two years old, and yet something of a veteran. A Londoner, he had passed out as a pilot at Cranwell on 16 February 1941.

A spell at 14 OTU at Cottesmore in Rutland followed, where F/L Nettleton checked him out for his Hampden solo. Nettleton, eleven months hence, would lead the epic daylight raid by elements of 44 and 97 Squadrons against the MAN diesel works at Augsburg, and be awarded the Victoria Cross as a result. In July 1941 Hopgood was posted to 50 Squadron to begin his operational career, and flew his first sortie to Bremen on 12 July as navigator to a F/O Abbott.

The fighter-style single-seat cockpit of the Hampden precluded a second pilot's position, and it became standard practice for the navigator/bomb-aimer's role to be undertaken by a qualified pilot. After operating once more with F/O Abbott, Hopgood carried out eight more Hampden sorties as navigator/bomb-aimer to a P/O Smith, before being posted to 25

OTU at Finningley at the end of October. While still with 25 OTU he began converting to Manchesters at Bircotes, and it was here that he came into contact with P/O Whamond, one of the future main stays of 106 Squadron. On 17 February 1942 Hopgood was signed off as a qualified Manchester pilot by W/C Lynch-Blosse, soon to be killed in action on his first sortie as commander of 44 (Rhodesia) Squadron. Hopgood was posted to Coningsby to join 106 Squadron, commanded at the time, as stated earlier, by W/C Allen. No 106 Squadron was already recognised as one of 5 Group's finest units, and over the ensuing year its reputation would flourish under its new commander. Hopgood's introduction to Manchester operations came as second pilot to Whamond on a mining sortie on 20 March, the day on which Gibson assumed command of the squadron. After two further operations as second pilot, he flew as captain of his own crew for the first time against Rostock on 23 April. No 106 Squadron was among the last in 5 Group to take on the ill-fated Manchester, but, thankfully, the type was approaching the end of its short period of service, and in May it was replaced by the Lancaster. It was Hopgood who saw Gibson safely through his conversion onto the type. Hopgood's first two Lancaster sorties were the thousand bomber raids against Cologne and Essen on 30/31 May and 1/2 June respectively. The former was an outstanding success, while the latter was an abysmal failure, but Hopgood came through both with flying colours. The remainder of his tour served to demonstrate his abilities, and it established his reputation as a first-rate pilot and captain. His press-on spirit ensured his status as a member of Gibson's inner circle, and the bond between the two men would prove to be fateful. Hopgood concluded his tour with 106 Squadron in October 1942 with a total of forty-six operations to his credit, and he was awarded the DFC on the 27th of that month. His next posting was to Station HQ Syerston in Nottinghamshire, where he carried out test flights in the new Hercules-powered Mk II Lancasters, and also instructed other pilots. This was followed by periods at the FIU at Ford and 148 5 Bombing Gunnery Flight at Fulbeck, where he flew half a dozen different types on various duties. He was awarded a Bar to his DFC on 11 January 1943. This sojourn ended on 29 March, when he flew to Scampton, and officially joined the newly formed 617 Squadron under Gibson on the following day.

On 16 May, John Hopgood took off with Gibson and Martin in a loose vic formation at 2139 hours. He was entrusted with the responsibility of acting as Gibson's deputy at the Möhne Dam in the event of Gibson's loss.

'He opened the hatch in the floor, and saw with alarm the close proximity of the tree-tops. Unless the chute opened instantly he was a dead man.'

As it turned out, Gibson survived while Hopgood did not. As the first to attack, Gibson had the element of surprise on his side. The German gunners realised they were the object of attention, but until Gibson's Lancaster thundered towards them, they didn't know if they were simply a navigation pinpoint or the intended target. They certainly had no inkling of how the attack would be pressed forward and from which direction. Gibson provided them with all the answers, and when Hopgood (as the second to attack) began his fourteen-second run across the lake towards the centre of the dam at 0033 hours, the gunners knew what to expect. It wasn't the first time Hopgood had been fired upon that night. Flak batteries around Dülmen had scored hits, leaving the wireless operator, John Minchin, with a severe leg wound. Minchin unpacked his parachute within the confines of his cramped compartment and tucked it under his arm. He opened the hatch in the floor, and saw with alarm the close proximity of the tree-tops. Unless the chute opened instantly he was a dead man. He knelt at the edge of the aperture and as he rolled forward he sensed the silk being snatched from his grasp by the slipstream. The tail wheel whistled past his head as he tumbled, and then the canopy filled with air and arrested his fall. After the briefest descent he felt the hard earth meet him. Meanwhile, Tony Burcher had managed to extricate himself from the rear turret to reach his parachute. He was confronted with the sight of John Minchin crawling along the fuselage with a leg almost cut through. Burcher ensured his friend's parachute was firmly attached before pushing him through the rear door and holding onto the rip-chord. Sadly, it was in

A Luftwaffe officer stands amidst the shattered remains of John Hopgood's Lancaster near the village of Ostönnen a few kilometres beyond the Möhne Dam. HELMUT EULER

A small memorial post bearing a brass plaque, indicating the area in which Hopgood's Lancaster crashed. Right: Hopgood's grave at Rheinberg.

doorway the aircraft was rent by an explosion as the fuel tank went up. Burcher was blasted into space and his back was hit a glancing blow by the tail plane. He landed heavily and was unable to walk, but he was alive. The shattered and burning remnants of the Lancaster fell out of the sky into a field at Ostönnen, six kilometres beyond the dam, and the bodies of Hopgood, Brennan, Earnshaw and Gregory were recovered by the Germans later that day.

TOUR GUIDE

To find the crash site we travel along the A44 (E331) from the direction of Dortmund towards Kassel until reaching exit 56 (Soest/Möhnesee). At the junction we turn left onto the B229 heading towards Delecke / Möhnesee. We follow this road until reaching a large crossroads, at which we will see a sign for the Bismarkturm. Here the B229 is intersected by the B516. We turn right onto the B516 towards Werl. We follow the B516 as far as a roundabout, which is an intersection with the L745. We turn right onto the L745 in the direction of Ostönnen. We follow this road until shortly before an underpass leading back beneath the A44 (E331). A narrow right-hand turn just before the underpass takes us to a track on the left. We leave the car at this point and go on foot along the track towards the nearby motorway. After a few metres we come across a wooden post bearing a brass plaque. This is the closest convenient point to the crash site of Hopgood's Lancaster, which, it is believed, fell approximately where the motorway now stands.

vain. Whether the gallant Minchin died as a result of his injuries or the fall is not known. Burcher strapped on his own chute and unpacked it as Fraser had done, then he plugged into the intercom to tell Hopgood he was leaving. Hopgood knew only seconds remained before the Lancaster tore itself apart, and he screamed at Burcher to get out. As the rear gunner stood in the

F/L W ASTELL

ED864, AJ-B NEAR MARBECK, NORTH OF RAESFELD

Earmarked to be S/L Young's deputy as A Flight commander at 617 Squadron, William (Bill) Astell was born in 1920 at Peover in Cheshire to an upper-class family. By the 1930s the family was resident in Chapel-en-le-Frith on the edge of the Peak District of Derbyshire.

His father, Godfrey, was the managing director of J & N Philips, a textile company, which he ran from its main site in Church Street, Manchester. His mother's sister was a member of the Dundas family, whose sons (and therefore Bill's cousins) John and Hugh flew Spitfires during the Battle of Britain. John was killed, but Hugh survived to become the RAF's youngest ever Group Captain, and as Sir Hugh he became Chairman of the BET Group and Thames television during the 1980s.

The Astell family's affluence enabled Bill to travel extensively overseas to broaden his education and

experience, and in 1936, at the age of sixteen, he sailed to Canada to visit relatives. He also took a trip to the White Sea in a trawler. He spent the end of 1937, most of 1938 and the first half of 1939 in Germany and France, and on his return to England he joined the RAF Air Reserve, undergoing training at an airfield in nearby Staffordshire. In September 1939 he was posted to Hastings to continue his training, before being posted to Salisbury, Southern Rhodesia, at the end of April 1940. He was awarded his wings in January 1941, passing out as a Pilot Officer, and he was immediately posted for duty in Malta. Before he had an opportunity to see action in the war, however, he was struck down by typhoid, and was forced to spend time first in hospital and then convalescing.

He finally joined 148 Squadron at Kabrit in Egypt in May 1941 and began operations as a Wellington pilot, attacking ports and landing grounds. A crash on 30 November left him with burns to his body, mostly his back, and cuts to his scalp and face, and although he did not consider himself to be seriously injured, he remained in hospital until February 1942. This was followed by a month's sick leave, which he spent in Kenya, before returning to duty with 148 Squadron and a new crew in March.

On the last night of May 1942, Astell took off to attack an enemy landing ground and failed to return, triggering the obligatory telegram to his family. Five days later Astell walked in to report being attacked by an enemy fighter over the target. Apart from wounding two of his crew, the engagement left his Wellington with an unserviceable rear turret and rudder controls, and a fire in the fuselage, starboard wing and engine nacelle. He ordered his crew to bale out, and four of them had time to comply before they ran out of altitude. Astell pulled off a crash-landing, and he and his navigator, P/O 'Bishop' Dodds, a former cleric, emerged from the wreckage with minor burns and began walking. After a few days a British patrol was spotted, and Astell moved forward to make contact, leaving his now ailing navigator hidden. He failed to make contact on this occasion, and was unable to relocate his navigator when he went back for him. Two days later Astell was picked up by Arabs and pointed in the direction of the British lines. He spent a few days in hospital in Tobruk, before being sent home via America, arriving back in England aboard the *Queen Mary* in September.

He was posted to Wigsley in Nottinghamshire, one of 5 Group's training stations, and also spent time at Hullavington and Fulbeck. Now with the rank of Flight Lieutenant, he was posted to 57 Squadron at Scampton on 25 January 1943 to undertake a second tour, this time on Lancasters, and it was here that he acquired his new crew. Operations followed to Milan, Nuremberg, Cologne, Berlin, Hamburg and Essen. After grabbing some sleep on return from the last mentioned on the night of 5/6 March, he went home on leave for what turned out to be the last time during his 57 Squadron service.

He returned to his squadron on 12 March and was posted to 617 Squadron on 25 March, not knowing what lay ahead. He managed one more spell of leave during the Dams training period, and while visiting his father at work, he accidentally ran into one of the secretaries, knocking her over and scattering papers over the floor. Picking her up he kissed her on the cheek, telling her he would see her on his next leave, with the prospect of that occurring after the operation for which they were preparing. All who knew Astell, particularly those of the fairer sex, would testify to his open, friendly, charming nature, which made him immensely likeable.

Astell's crew was fairly typical of those posted in as founder members of 617 Squadron, and it is interesting to delve a little more deeply into their individual backgrounds as representative of the squadron as a whole. Five of the crew had been together at 1654 Conversion Unit (CU) at Wigsley from October 1942 until their posting to 9 Squadron at Waddington two days before Christmas. They were navigator Floyd Wile, bomb-aimer Don Hopkinson, wireless operator Al Garshowitz and gunners Frank Garbas and Richard Bolitho. At Waddington they were teamed up with a Sgt Stephenson as their pilot, with whom they flew for the first time on Christmas Eve, carrying out circuits and landings. This association was not destined to last long, however, although Sgt Stephenson's disappearance from the scene is a little confusing. On the night of 8/9 January 1943 a 9 Squadron Lancaster failed to return from a raid on Duisburg, and Sgt Foote and his crew were all killed. Listed as the crew's flight engineer was Sgt M W Stephenson, who is assumed to be the pilot mentioned above. In 9 Squadron records, though, he is shown as a flight engineer, and not as a pilot flying as second dickey. There were seven men on board the missing Lancaster, not eight as was normal when a second pilot was being carried. Sgt Foote's regular flight engineer was not on the trip, and this leaves us with the conclusion that, if these Stephensons are one and the same, he must have volunteered to act as flight engineer at short notice. Had he survived, matters might have turned out differently for his former crew.

FLOYD WILE

Floyd Wile was one of three Canadians in the crew. He was born in Nova Scotia in April 1919, the fifth of seven children. Following high school he worked on the land as a farm hand and in the lumber industry. He had shown an interest in radio during his youth and actually studied the subject for a year at technical school. He was also keen on sporting activities, particularly skiing, skating and swimming. Before enlisting in the RCAF he joined a local army unit in Yarmouth, Nova Scotia, but resigned after a month. At 5 Initial Training School he was noted as being slow thinking, hard working – the plodder type; while at No 8 Air Observer School he was described as average, with the comment, *'in no respect has he shown much aptitude for work'*. Another report described him as a quiet lad, and backward through lack of experience in mixing. Three months later, however, his commanding officer at No 9 Bombing and Gunnery School called him outstanding and a brilliant trainee, who was very popular and had good self control. Despite this he passed out of No 2 Air Navigation School with a *'not outstanding, average NCO material'* tag, but was commissioned as a Pilot Officer before leaving Wigsley in December 1942.

ABRAM GARSHOWITZ

The other Canadians in Astell's crew were Abram Garshowitz (known within his family as Albert or Al) and Frank Garbas, who were great boyhood friends. Al was the ninth of twelve children, and was born in Hamilton, Ontario, in December 1921. He went to school locally, and afterwards worked in the family business selling new and used furniture. Frank Garbas was born in July 1922, ten years after his parents arrived in Canada from their native Poland. He was the fifth of nine children. Once in Canada the letter 'z' was dropped from the family name Garbasz, while his father became Stanley rather than Stanislaus. Even so, family life revolved around Polish traditions, religion and cuisine, and Polish was the dominant language spoken at home. Frank was a gentle, quiet person, who was very close to his mother, and also, as mentioned, to Al Garshowitz, with whom he played semi-pro American football with the Eastwood Lions before enlisting in the RCAF, having worked briefly for Otis, the elevator manufacturers.

DONALD HOPKINSON

Donald Hopkinson was born at Royton, Oldham, in Lancashire in September 1920 as a second child. Just four months later his mother died of cancer, and Donald went to live with his grandfather, and an aunt, uncle and cousin. After his father remarried, a half brother and two half sisters were added to his family. A keen cricketer, Donald attended grammar school in Royton, before working in the office of the local Co-operative Society. He enlisted in the RAF in December 1941.

RICHARD BOLITHO

Richard Bolitho was born in Portrush, County Antrim, in January 1920, but was brought to England early on by his parents, who kept a hotel in Nottingham. Richard eventually moved in with his aunt, who ran a grocery shop in Kimberley, but after her death, his father

sold the hotel and took over the shop. After attending school in nearby Heanor, Don worked for Ericcsons Telephones at Beeston, and enlisted in the RAF in November 1940.

JOHN KINNEAR

The final member of the crew, flight engineer John Kinnear, did not become involved with Astell and the others until they had already carried out four operations with 57 Squadron. He was born in Fife, Scotland, in November 1921, and grew up to be a likeable, carefree young man who was mad about flying. He worked as a mechanic until he was old enough to enlist, and this he did in 1939. He was at 1654 Conversion Unit at the same time as the other members of his future crew, but does not appear to have arrived at 57 Squadron until later. He flew his first operations with the crew against Hamburg on the night of 3/4 March 1943 and Essen two nights later.

Astell wrote home for the last time on 14 May, and although tension must have been growing at Scampton, he took pains to keep any hint of it from his family. He enclosed a copy of his will, joking that the RAF takes on some funny ideas in telling all squadron members to make one. He closed by saying, *'There is no news at all from here. Lovely weather and a very quiet life'*. Astell's will was witnessed by Henry Maudslay and Norm Barlow, and fate would decree that the lives of these three men and their crews would end within a few miles of each other in the flatlands of rural Germany between the Ruhr and the Dutch frontier a few days hence.

Astell took off from Scampton at 2159 along with S/L Henry Maudslay and P/O Les Knight as the final section of wave one. The three Lancasters remained in loose formation across the North Sea, heading for the gap

The charred remains of a crew member in the foreground (left of photograph), provides a stark and poignant image of war.

The wreckage of Astell's Lancaster lies in a field behind the Lammer's farm house.

between the islands of Schouwen and Walcheren in the Scheldt Estuary. All apparently proceeded according to plan until shortly after they crossed into Germany. As Maudslay and Knight made a course alteration, Astell continued on the original heading. It was only a brief parting of the ways and Astell soon found the correct track. He followed hard on the heels of his colleagues, perhaps a minute behind, two at the most. It is important to establish that Astell's deviation from track was not responsible in itself for the crash a few minutes later.

Eyewitnesses were awoken by the sound of two aircraft thundering over their rooftops. By the time they had got up and gone outside to investigate, Astell was upon them, colliding with an electricity pylon. This proves that Astell was following the same heading as the others and was at about the same altitude. After hitting the pylon, the Lancaster erupted in flames, scraped over the farmhouse and crashed a few seconds later in the field behind the neighbouring farmhouse. The bomb did not explode on contact, but rolled into the field, on fire, for about a hundred yards before it detonated. Perhaps the attention of Astell and his crew was focused ahead, searching in the distance for the tell tale glow of exhausts from the other Lancasters, and this was the reason that they failed to spot a hazard to aircraft while they were flying at the ultra low level that had been discussed at the pre-operational briefing. We will, of course, never know the real reason. The incident took place at about 0015 DBST, and ED864 was the third of the nineteen Lancasters of Operation *Chastise* to be lost before any of the targets had been reached. The pylon struck by Astell was repaired and remains to this day where it stood in 1943.

TOUR GUIDE

From Oberhausen or Gelsenkirchen we travel along the A2 (E34) as far as the Bottrop junction. Here we pick up the A31 in the direction of Gronau. We follow the A31 until exit 37 for Schermbeck. At the junction with the B58 we turn left towards the towns of Haltern and Raesfeld. We travel a short distance until meeting a major crossroads with traffic lights. We take a left onto the B224 and head for Raesfeld. We then follow the B224 into the centre of Raesfeld, where we join the B70 for Borken. We leave Raesfeld behind us and travel along a tree-lined rural stretch of the B70 still heading towards Borken. After we have travelled for a few minutes, and just after crossing the Döringbach (a small stream), to the right we see a farmhouse, and directly thereafter a narrow right-hand turn. We take that road as far as the first fork, where we bear left. Continue to the next fork and keep right. Continue, going over a crossroads, and eventually the road bends to the left heading due north. Shortly thereafter the Tücking farm appears on the left-hand side. We maintain our course, ignoring a road branching off to the right. We are now on narrow single-track roads linking the neighbouring farms. At the next crossroads we are at our destination. Immediately to our left is the Lammers' farmhouse and yard, and over our left shoulder the neighbouring Thesing house. Looking over the Thesing's roof we can see the top of the pylon struck by Astell's Lancaster. Turning right at this crossroads we have the crash site in the field on our left behind a high hedge. Maybe fifty or so metres further on is a gap in the hedge and a rampart across the ditch. Here you will find the stone and plaque mentioned above erected as a permanent memorial to F/L Astell and his crew who perished in this spot.

W/C G W HOLDEN

EE144, KC-S NORDHORN DORTMUND-EMS CANAL RAID

S/L George Holden, late of 4 Group, arrived at Scampton on 2 July 1943 to take up his duty as senior flight commander and squadron commander elect of 617 Squadron.

In April Holden had completed six months as an acting Wing Commander in command of 102 Squadron – 'Dinghy' Young's old unit. On 1 July, he flew to Scampton in an Anson, but his log book does not state whether or not he landed. He may simply have been taking a look from the air at his new home, before his posting there on the following day. It would be a further month before Gibson departed the squadron, and Holden needed time to learn the ways of the Lancaster, a type unfamiliar to him and to all others whose careers had been spent in 4 Group.

Holden was a 4 Group man to the core, and perhaps not an obvious choice to replace the charismatic Gibson, now the most celebrated squadron commander in the entire service. His selection actually began a trend of appointing 4 Group men to the position, such as Cheshire, Tait and Fauquier, men who would carry the squadron through to the end of the bombing war in late

April 1945. If Harris, and one might reasonably assume some involvement on his part, was prepared to look outside of 5 Group for Gibson's successor, why did he sanction the appointment of Holden from among the wealth of qualified existing squadron commanders available? It has to be said, that there was something of the Gibson character in Holden. His career to this point had been distinguished, and he had been involved in some unusual and spectacular operations. He had also rubbed shoulders with some of the Command's finest young bloods, many of whom were gathered within the squadrons of 4 Group, and were themselves seen as shining lights. Not all had survived to the summer of 1943, and of those who had (whose operational careers had begun in 1940), Holden was unquestionably among the brightest prospects. If Dinghy Young (a 4 Group contemporary of Holden and Cheshire) had survived, or perhaps even Henry Maudslay from the 'class of '41', then they would also undoubtedly have been in the

Guy Gibson at the time of handing command of 617 Squadron to W/C George Holden. In the picture also are the members of Gibson's Dams crew, four of whom died with Holden at Nordhorn on their way to the Dortmund-Ems Canal. 3rd from left: Taerum, 4th from left: Deering, 6th from left: Hutchison. 9th from left: Holden and 11th from left: Spafford. 5th from left: is Trevor-Roper, who was Gibson's rear gunner for Operation Chastise. He died in a Pathfinder Lancaster of 97 Squadron during the infamous Nuremberg raid of the 30/31st of March1944, when 95 heavy bombers failed to return. Gibson is 7th from the left, while 10th is Pulford, Gibson's much maligned flight engineer, who was killed in Bill Suggitt's Lancaster during a transit flight in February 1944.

frame, but they were gone. Cheshire had progressed to the rank of Group Captain, which generally speaking at that time, precluded him from the command of a squadron. This latter restriction was in the process of being revised, however, as Pathfinder squadrons were now being led by Group Captains, with Wing Commanders filling the roll of flight commander.

Holden began basic training, presumably part-time as a reservist, in May 1937. On 1 September 1939, the day German forces began their assault on Poland, he joined 9 Flying Training School at Hullavington, moved on to Benson between January and early May 1940, and thence to 10 Operational Training Unit (OTU) at Abingdon, where he learned to fly Whitleys. This was the type operated by 4 Group until the advent of the Halifax, and it would be the spring of 1942 before it was finally withdrawn from operational service with the Command. He passed out as a first pilot, day only, with an average rating on 18 September, and immediately joined 78 Squadron at Dishforth. Here, he began working up to operational status, and undertook his first sortie as second pilot to F/L Pattison in a raid on Antwerp on the night of 26/27 September. His second sortie was to Amsterdam with his flight commander, S/L Wildey, who would eventually take command of 10 Squadron, and lose his life in action in October 1942, the same month in which Holden would gain his first command. Finally, on 11 November, Holden was signed out as a fully qualified Whitley captain by the newly appointed commanding officer, W/C 'Charles' Whitworth. Two nights later he undertook his first operation as crew captain, his eighth sortie in all, but like many others operating in poor weather conditions that night, he was forced to abandon his sortie and return home. He put matters right on 15/16 November, however, when participating in an unusually effective raid on Hamburg.

Late in 1940, Prime Minister Churchill pressed for the formation of a paratroop unit, as the forerunner of an airborne force for use in a future invasion of Europe. Plans were put in hand to carry out a special operation under the code name Colossus, with the purpose of ascertaining the viability of such an undertaking. Volunteers were brought together as X-Troop No 11 SAS Battalion for an attack on an aqueduct over the River Tragino in Italy to be launched from Malta. Two aircraft were to carry out a diversionary bombing attack on marshalling yards at nearby Foggia, while six others delivered the parachutists into position. Nos 51 and 78 Squadrons each selected to provide four aircraft and crews under the command of W/C James Tait, who had recently begun a short spell as commanding officer of the former. Among the pilots from 78 Squadron was P/O Holden, who flew with Tait on a container-dropping test as part of the run-up on 2 February. On completion of their task the surviving commandos were to gather at a point on the coast for evacuation by submarine. The force departed for Malta on the night of 7/8 February, and carried out the operation on 10/11 February. In the event, not all of the commandos were dropped within

range of their target, and if this were not unfortunate enough, one of the diversionary Whitleys had to be abandoned in the area selected for the ground force's withdrawal, thus alerting the local defenders. Some damage was inflicted upon the aqueduct, but all of the soldiers were captured on their way to the rendezvous, and they were joined soon afterwards by the Whitley crew.

This operation was Holden's twentieth, and his last with 78 Squadron, which he left with an above average rating to join 35 Squadron at Linton-on-Ouse. No 35 Squadron had been reformed at Boscombe Down in November 1940 to introduce the Halifax into operational service, and was attracting the leading bomber pilots in 4 Group. Holden arrived on 25 February 1941, and met up again with Tait, who had now reverted to Squadron Leader rank and was a flight commander under the portly personage of the squadron commander, W/C R W P Collings, another of the Command's great characters. The Halifax suffered many teething problems, and the demand for modifications ensured only a trickle of new aircraft from the factories. As a result, following its operational baptism in March, the type operated only intermittently and in very small numbers for some time.

Holden flew his first Halifax sortie against Duisburg on 11/12 June, and over the ensuing five weeks managed ten more. A major assault on the German cruisers *Scharnhorst, Gneisenau* and *Prinz Eugen* at Brest, the first two-named having been in residence there since the end of March, was planned for 24 July. The operation was to be undertaken in daylight by Halifaxes accompanied by 1 and 3 Group Wellingtons, and under extensive diversionary activity and a heavy fighter escort. It was discovered at the eleventh hour, however, that the *Scharnhorst* had slipped away to La Pallice, some two hundred miles further south, and it was decided to send the Halifax element after her, while the remainder of the original plan went ahead at Brest. Fifteen Halifaxes from 35 and 76 Squadrons duly attacked the *Scharnhorst*, causing extensive damage, but lost five of their number in the process, and all of the surviving aircraft sustained damage to some degree. Holden was forced to bring his bombs home after flak shot away the electrical release gear. One of his crew was killed, while two others were wounded, one seriously. Holden's flight commander at the time was S/L Jimmy Marks, one of the brightest stars in Bomber Command. Marks would gain command of 35 Squadron in 1942, only to lose his life in action shortly after taking the Squadron into the Pathfinder Force as one of the founder units.

Holden concluded his tour with a total of thirty-two operations, and was posted to the Heavy Conversion Flight at Linton-on-Ouse on 18 August. Here he remained until December, when he was detached to Upavon, before progressing to Marston Moor, Leeming and Pocklington in the role of instructor. At Pocklington, and now with the rank of Squadron Leader, he was put in charge of the Conversion Flight of 405 Squadron, a

Canadian unit commanded by W/C Johnny Fauquier. While there, Holden flew on the second thousand bomber raid against Essen on 1/2 June 1942, and the third and final one on Bremen on 25/26 June, his thirty-third and thirty-fourth sorties. In July he was posted to 158 Squadron's Conversion Flight at East Moor, where he remained until 25 October. In the early hours of the previous day, 102 Squadron's commanding officer, W/C Bintley, had been killed in a freak accident on the runway at Holme-on-Spalding-Moor on return from Genoa, when another Halifax had crushed his cockpit on landing. Holden was posted as his replacement on 25th, and began a successful period of command, during which he operated a further eleven times, bringing his tally to forty-five. He was rested again on 20 April 1943, and thereafter seemed to kick his heels somewhat until the call came through from 617 Squadron. On 4 July, two days after his arrival at Scampton, he was taken up by Martin in EE148 for a local familiarisation trip, and the two paired up again on the following two days. On 7 July Holden flew with Gibson's Dams crew for the first time. W/C Holden was confirmed as the new commanding officer on 2 August, Gibson's final day on the squadron. The pair enjoyed a 1 hour 25 minute farewell cross-country flight together in ED933 with Gibson's crew, soon to be Holden's crew, in attendance.

A commanding officer's crew possessed a certain status, despite the fact that Gibson's was a disparate bunch who had come together for the first time at Scampton, and had thus far completed only the Dams operation as the crew of the CO. Two of them, 'Terry' Taerum, a Canadian, and Fred 'Spam' Spafford from Australia, arrived via the 50 Squadron academy and 1654 Conversion Unit, while the wireless operator, Bob Hutchison,was well known to Gibson, having completed a tour with 106 Squadron. The front gunner, George Deering, whom Gibson described in *Enemy Coast Ahead* as 'green', had actually completed a first tour, and Operation *Chastise* would be his thirty-sixth sortie. His previous operations had been undertaken on Wellingtons with 1 Group's 103 Squadron, which he joined from 21 OTU on 16 August 1941. After screening he went to 22 OTU, on 11 May 1942, and took part in one or more of the thousand bomber raids. Of the other members of Gibson's Dams crew, flight engineer John Pulford remained with the squadron until losing his life in a Lancaster crash in February 1944, and the rear gunner, Richard Trevor-Roper, was eventually posted to the Pathfinder's 97 Squadron, and was killed in action during the catastrophic Nuremberg raid at the end of March 1944. As a replacement for Pulford, Holden chose Dennis Powell, who had flown to the dams with Townsend. For the Dortmund-Ems Canal operation each Lancaster would carry an eight-man crew, so that each turret could be manned. To facilitate this a number of gunners were temporarily posted in from training units. The two final members of Holden's crew, the mid-upper and rear gunners, were respectively F/O Pringle and P/O Meikle.

Holden took off from Coningsby at 2356 hours at the

head of the first wave. Following in his prop wash were Martin, Knight and Wilson They remained in close contact until reaching the town of Nordhorn, some twenty miles – seven minutes' flying time – from the rendezvous point at Wettringen. In their path stood a church, and Holden elected to climb over it rather than go round. This was probably an instinctive decision taken by a man who had spent his extensive operational career believing that H-E-I-G-H-T spelt safety. In contrast, for those who had been at 617 Squadron since the start, low flying had become a way of life. Martin, Knight and Wilson instinctively remained at rooftop height and simply changed course to miss the church. Holden's decision to climb to perhaps 300 feet presented his aircraft in profile to a lone light-flak gun on a factory roof over to starboard. Only a few shells were fired, but at least one punctured a wing tank and set the Lancaster ablaze. Within seconds it had flipped over and nosed into the ground about half a mile from the town centre. The fiercely burning wreckage lay only yards from a farmhouse containing Herr and Frau Hood and six of their children. The youngsters were sheltering in the cellar, and the parents ventured up into the house to collect night-clothes. It was then, after some fifteen minutes' of cooking in the blazing wreckage, that the bomb went up, flattening the house and all of the other buildings in the farmyard. Somehow Herr Hood survived, but the remains of his wife were found under the rubble when daylight came. She proved to be the only German fatality on a night of heavy loss for 617 Squadron. The explosion shattered windows and stripped tiles from roofs within a half-mile radius.

TOUR GUIDE
Travelling from the direction of Osnabrück we journey along the A30 (E30) towards the Dutch frontier. We leave the A30 (E30) at Junction 3 Nordhorn/Bad Bentheim. The slip road leads onto the B403. We turn left onto this road and head for Nordhorn. Before Nordhorn the B403 and B213 merge as one under the name Osttangente. We remain on the Osttangente as far as the exit for the Frensdorfer Ring, in the direction of Nordhorn. We turn right onto the Frensdorfer Ring and cross back over Osttangente as if heading into Nordhorn. Now take the second exit on the right shortly after the flyover we have just passed, and this brings us onto a narrow road. We follow this road and take the first left. We park the car with the Vechta Lake in front of us at the point where a footpath leads us to the right. This brings us automatically past the farmhouse and yard of the Hood family. It was here that W/C Holden's Lancaster impacted the ground. When the bomb detonated it completely destroyed the house. The house we see today is a reconstruction.

ROLL OF HONOUR

Those Who Lost Their Lives During Operation *Chastise* and on the Dortmund-Ems Canal

KEY: (C) – RCAF • (A) – RAAF • (NZ) – RNZAF • * – BAR • MID – MENTIONED IN DISPATCHES

Operation *Chastise* 16/17 May 1943

LANCASTER ED934 AJ-K

Pilot: P/O V W Byers (C)
Flight engineer: Sgt A J Taylor
Navigator: P/O J H Warner
Wireless operator: Sgt J Wilkinson
Bomb-aimer: Sgt A N Whitaker
Front gunner: Sgt J McA Jarvie
Rear gunner: Sgt J McDowell (C)

LANCASTER ED864 AJ-B

Pilot: F/L W Astell DFC
Flight engineer: Sgt J Kinnear
Navigator: P/O F A Wile (C)
Wireless operator: Sgt A Garshowitz (C)
Bomb-aimer: F/O D Hopkinson
Front gunner: Sgt F A Garbas (C)
Rear gunner: Sgt R Bolitho

LANCASTER ED927 AJ-E

Pilot: F/L R N G Barlow DFC(A)
Flight engineer: Sgt S L Whillis

Navigator: F/O P S Burgess
Wireless operator: F/O C R Williams DFC (A)
Bomb-aimer: Sgt A Gillespie DFM
Front gunner: F/O H S Glinz (C)
Rear gunner: Sgt J R G Liddell

LANCASTER ED925 AJ-M

Pilot: F/L J V Hopgood DFC*
Flight engineer: Sgt C Brennan
Navigator: F/O K Earnshaw (C)
Wireless operator: Sgt J W Minchin
Front gunner: P/O G H F G Gregory DFM

LANCASTER ED865 AJ-S

Pilot: P/O L J Burpee DFM (C)
Flight engineer: Sgt G Pegler
Navigator: Sgt T Jaye
Wireless operator: P/O L G Weller
Bomb-aimer: Sgt J L Arthur (C)
Front gunner: Sgt W C A Long
Rear gunner: F/S J G Brady (C)

LANCASTER ED910 AJ-C

Pilot: P/O W Ottley DFC
Flight engineer: Sgt R Marsden
Navigator: F/O J K Barrett DFC
Wireless operator: Sgt J Guterman DFM
Bomb-aimer: F/S T B Johnston
Front gunner: Sgt H J Strange

LANCASTER ED937 AJ-Z

Pilot: S/L H E Maudslay DFC
Flight engineer: Sgt J Marriott DFM
Navigator: F/O R A Urquhart DFC (C)
Wireless operator: Sgt L W Nichols
Bomb-aimer: P/O M J D Fuller
Front gunner: F/O W J Tytherleigh DFC
Rear gunner: Sgt J R Burrows

LANCASTER ED887 AJ-A

Pilot: S/L H M Young DFC*
Flight engineer: Sgt D T Horsfall
Navigator: Sgt C W Roberts
Wireless operator: Sgt A P Cottam (C)
Bomb-aimer: F/O V S MacCausland (C)
Front gunner: Sgt G A Yeo
Rear gunner: Sgt W Ibbotson

Dortmund-Ems Canal 14/15 September 1943 (Aborted)

LANCASTER JA981 KC-J

Pilot: S/L D J H Maltby DSO DFC
Flight engineer: Sgt W Hatton
Navigator: F/S V Nicholson DFM
Wireless operator: F/S A J Stone
Bomb-aimer: P/O J Fort DFC
Gunner: W/O J L Welch DFM
Gunner: H T Simmonds

Dortmund-Ems Canal 15/16 September 1943

LANCASTER EE144 AJ-S

Pilot: W/C G W Holden DSO DFC* MID
Flight engineer: Sgt D J D Powell MID
Navigator: F/L T H Taerum DFC (C)
Wireless operator: F/L R E G Hutchison DFC*
Bomb-aimer: F/O F M Spafford DFC DFM (A)
Gunner: P/O G A Deering DFC (C)
Gunner: F/O H J Pringle DFC
Gunner: P/O T A Meikle DFM

LANCASTER EE130 AJ-A

Pilot: F/L R A P Allsebrook DSO DFC
Flight engineer: F/S P Moore

Navigator: P/O N A Botting
Wireless operator: F/O J M Grant DFC
Bomb-aimer: F/S R B S Lulham
Gunner: Sgt I G Jones
Gunner: F/S W Walker
Gunner: F/S S Hitchen

LANCASTER JA874 KC-E

Pilot: P/O W G Divall
Flight engineer: Sgt E C A Blake
Navigator: F/O D W Warwick (C)
Wireless operator: F/S J S Simpson
Bomb-aimer: F/S R C McArthur
Gunner: Sgt A A Williams
Gunner: Sgt G S Miles
Gunner: Sgt D Allatson

LANCASTER JA898 KC-X

Pilot: F/L H S Wilson
Flight engineer: P/O T W Johnson
Navigator: F/O J A Rodger
Wireless operator: W/O L Mieyette (C)
Bomb-aimer: F/O G H Coles (C)
Gunner: F/S T H Payne
Gunner: Sgt G M Knox
Gunner: F/S E Hornby

LANCASTER JB144 KC-N

Pilot: F/L L G Knight DSO MID (A)

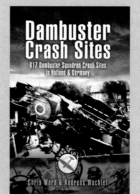

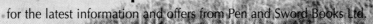

'Two mighty walls of water were last night rolling irresistibly down the Ruhr and Eder valleys. Railway bridges, power stations, factories whole villages and built-up areas were being swept away.'

AFTER THE DAMS RAID

The RAF Museum in Hendon has a file of press cuttings about Operation *Chastise*, all neatly pasted into what advertising agencies call a 'guard book'. This is a large format cloth-bound book with leaves made of stiff grey paper, and is designed to keep a permanent record of newspaper and magazine advertising.

By Charles Foster

This article was extracted from *Breaking The Dams - The Story of Dambuster David Maltby and His Crew* and is reproduced here by permission of Pen and Sword Books Ltd.

Turning over the pages of this book, you get a real idea of the impact that the Dams Raid must have made on the British people starting to think that the war was going their way. The Allies had had a run of success over the previous few months with El Alamein in November 1942 and the final Soviet victory in Stalingrad in February 1943 heralded as great triumphs.

After Alamein, Churchill once more found words which seemed to capture the mood:

'this is not the end, it is not even the beginning of the end. But it is, perhaps, the end of the beginning.'

Winston Churchill.

Now, a day or two after news of the final Allied victory in Tunisia had reached Britain, which meant that plans for the invasion of Sicily and then Italy could go ahead, this daring raid on the dams in the Ruhr valleys captured the public's imagination. Nowadays we would call the press and public relations operation mounted by the Air Ministry and the Ministry of Information 'spin', with all

the pejorative overtones that that implies, but there is no doubt that the press was given substantial help in the production of their stories, including the release of the dramatic reconnaissance photographs. Of course in war time, with no opportunity to check material and with the only foreign reports coming from neutral Switzerland, Sweden and Spain, it is completely understandable that the press should carry what the official sources wanted them to say.

This would explain why some of the details were either wrong or based on speculation. *The Daily Telegraph*, for instance, informed its readers that 'three key dams' had been blown up, while the *Daily Mirror* was more sensationalist, with a headline reading *'Huns get a flood blitz: torrent rages along Ruhr'*. The *Daily Mail* ran a headline over its photographs: *'The Smash-Up: RAF Picture Testifies to Perfect Bombing'*. Its story went on:

'Two mighty walls of water were last night

The breached wall of the Sorpe dam.

Flood devastation to railways and property caused by the huge amount of water from the broken dams.

out was explained thus:

> *The bomber crews' tricky task was to drop 1,500 lb mines in a confined area inside the torpedo net... in the centre of the dam, where the current would draw them down towards the sluice gates and explode them there. The attack had to be made with perfect coolness, and the mines dropped from a height of sometimes less than 100ft.*

This cover story was dreamed up by the Air Ministry for public consumption, and Gibson was to describe the same fictional technique on his later US and Canadian lecture tour. The intelligence services weren't to know that concealing the details of the mine was futile: the Germans had already recovered an unexploded Upkeep mine (from the crashed aircraft of Flt Lt Barlow) and were busy working out its secrets even as these articles were appearing in the press.

The King and Queen's visit to Scampton ten days after the raid (which was carefully described as 'an air station in the north of England') and the list of decorations which accompanied it prompted another round of press interest. This brought about the first use of the word 'dam-buster', which appears on the day of the royal visit, 27 May 1943, in a small headline in the *Daily Mirror: 'Dam-buster Gibson to get V C.'* The *Mirror* (perhaps the same anonymous sub-editor on another evening shift?) was obviously quite pleased with its new word, as it was used a couple of times again in the week following, and other papers such as the *Daily Sketch* soon followed suit.

It wasn't just the national and international press who covered the raid. Local papers also became involved. The arrival home on leave of AJ-J's flight engineer, Bill Hatton, was noted by the *Wakefield Express* under the heading '*A Wakefield Hero*'. Readers were informed that he had taken part '*in the great raid on the German dams*'.

rolling irresistibly down the Ruhr and Eder valleys. Railway bridges, power stations, factories, whole villages and built-up areas were being swept away.'

Flicking through the guard book, I saw how the coverage lasted for days, fed by further information coming from the Air Ministry, as the floods spread further and further down the valleys. '*Havoc spreads hour by hour*' one paper recorded, and there was speculation that the third dam might burst at any moment. The weekly magazines got in on the act at the end of the week, and the following week as well, with an extraordinary double page spread 'artist's impression' in the *Illustrated London News* of '*how the raid was carried out*'. This was drawn by no less a person than the 'celebrated aviation artist' Captain Bryan de Grineau '*from information given by the Air Ministry*'. In it, a Lancaster is shown flying along the length of the Möhne Dam, not directly towards it, which is what actually happened. The way in which the operation was carried

The front cover of The Daily Sketch *breaking the news of the Dambuster success.*

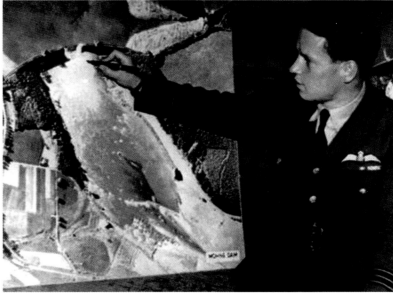

Left: An RAF aerial photograph of the bomb damage and Above: Guy signing his name across the breach in the Möhne Dam.

When it came out, the list of decorations was pretty astonishing. Of the seventy-seven airmen who returned from the raid, thirty-four were awarded an honour of one sort or another, with Guy Gibson receiving the highest bravery award of all, the Victoria Cross. More than half the personnel in the crews who succeeded in both bombing and getting home safely were decorated. (Two crews had to make an early return after their

'More than half the personnel in the crews who succeeded in both bombing and getting home safely were decorated.'

aircraft were damaged on the outward flight.)

Amongst those decorated were three crew members from AJ-J (piloted by Squadron Leader David Maltby). Like all the crews who dropped their mines successfully, the pilot, navigator and bomb aimer were decorated. A strict pecking order was followed: officer pilots were awarded a Distinguished Service Order (DSO), the two non-

No one seems sure who to follow as a large group of newly decorated 617 Squadron personnel march away outside Buckingham Palace. David Maltby is sixth from the left, John Fort is fourth from the right.

" Dam Busters ": By Cuthbert Orde
Some of the Men Who Destroyed the Ruhr Dams

F/Lt. D. J. Shannon, D.S.O., D.F.C.

P/O. K. W. Brown, C.G.M.

P/O. W. C. Townsend, C.G.M., D.F.M.

F/Lt. H. B. Martin, D.S.O., D.F.C.

F/Lt. J. C. McCarthy, D.S.O., D.F.C.

S/Ldr. D. J. H. Maltby, D.S.O., D.F.C.

W/Cdr. G. P. Gibson, V.C., D.S.O., D.F.C.

F/Lt. R. D. Trevor-Roper, D.F.C., D.F.M.

Double page spread from The Tatler, 1 September 1943, featuring Cuthbert Orde's drawings.

PHOTO: FAMILY COLLECTION

commissioned pilots got the equivalent CGM – the Conspicuous Gallantry Medal (Flying). All the other officers got Distinguished Flying Crosses (DFC), while the other sergeants and flight sergeants got Distinguished Flying Medals (DFM).

There is something of a mystery as to why the medals were divided out in this way. The only aircraft where all seven members were decorated was Gibson's. That's understandable enough, but why six of Bill Townsend's crew (all except the poor old flight engineer) got medals is not at all clear. They had a difficult enough flight, arriving back last of all, and were the only crew who bombed the Ennepe Dam – but it didn't breach. When front gunner Sgt Douglas Webb got a telegram about his medal, he thought at first it was a practical joke. (Of all the Operation *Chastise* survivors, Doug Webb had one of the most remarkable post-war careers. He went back to working in Fleet Street as a photographer and then branched out into film stills and 'glamour' work. It was while doing this work that he took the first nude pictures of the celebrated model and actress Pamela Green, while she was still a schoolgirl. In the 1950s and 60s she made a career out of glamour work, culminating in the naturist picture

'The draft citations make interesting reading, as well as being riddled with typing errors.'

Naked as Nature Intended. Her straight acting career included the 1960 Michael Powell film *Peeping Tom* where the moderately explicit shots of her got local watch committees in a fuss. Doug Webb was to marry Pamela Green in 1967. They later retired to the Isle of Wight, where she still lives after his death in 1996.)

So, David Maltby was awarded a DSO to add to the DFC he had received nine months before, while John Fort got a DFC and Vivian Nicholson a DFM. The draft citations make interesting reading, as well as being riddled with typing errors. (The strain of preparing thirty-four citations must have told on the typist, as these are not the only ones that occurred.) Vivian is called 'Victor' (although as his medal was engraved Sgt V Nicholson, perhaps this didn't matter too much). David's middle name is spelt 'Hatfield', a common error, and he is wrongly allocated twenty-eight operations, when *Chastise* was actually his twenty-ninth. John Fort's rank varies between Pilot Officer and Flying Officer in the course of two pages. His promotion, when it came through later, was backdated to 15 March 1943, so technically the higher rank is correct. What is astonishing are the hours flown and the number of operations. Here it is in black and white:

Vivian had flown operational hours of 5 hours and 40 minutes in just one operation; John for 9 hours and 40 minutes in two. They were, by far, the most inexperienced of the thirty-four decorated aircrew in 617 Squadron, and Vivian was probably the youngest.

The recommendation reads:

PARTICULARS OF MERITORIOUS SERVICE

Flight Lieutenant Maltby (Pilot), Sergeant Nicholson (Navigator) and Pilot Officer Fort (Air Bomber) were part of the crew of an aircraft which was detailed to attack the Möhne Dam. By an extremely high standard of crew co-operation, and by showing the greatest sense of duty in the face of heavy opposition and other difficulties, this crew succeeded in making the final breach in the Möhne Dam.

I strongly recommend the immediate award of the Distinguished Service Order to F/Lt Maltby, and the Distinguished Flying Cross to P/O Fort, and of the Distinguished Flying Medal to Sgt Nicholson.

The recommendations were signed by Whitworth. Over the page Cochrane and Harris added their signatures concurring in the awards.

When the King and Queen came to Scampton, each crew was lined up behind their captain, who stood smartly to attention, toe-caps touching a white line painted on the grass. Gibson introduced the King to each of the pilots. Some sources say that the pilots each then introduced the rest of his crew, but this is at odds with what can be seen from the few seconds shown on the newsreels and the accounts of Len Sumpter and Fred Sutherland, who said that they did not. An official RAF photographer recorded the scene, and shot some of the pictures in colour. When you are so used to seeing wartime pictures in black and white the rich Kodachrome

process is almost shockingly bright.

Most of the shots show the King and Queen talking to the pilots. In the one of Shannon, Vivian Nicholson can be seen in the distance, eyes front, at attention behind David. Talking to David, the King seems to be asking him a question, and David looks nervous as he gropes for an answer. Curiously, he is still only wearing a Flight Lieutenant's two rings on his sleeve. The inner half-ring indicating his promotion to Squadron Leader ten days previously has not yet been added.

David's promotion to Squadron Leader and role as the Commander of A Flight meant a lot of bureaucratic work, planning schedules and countersigning logbooks. On 2 June he took over temporary command of the squadron while Gibson was on leave. The flight authorisation books show that intensive training was going on during this time. Flights averaging about two hours took place almost every day, to familiar training locations such as the lake at Uppingham or the bombing ranges at Wainfleet.

But there was no word yet about what Bomber Command planned to do with the squadron. This gave time for the squadron to support Gibson in his growing public relations role. Gibson was sent off to places such as Sheffield, Gloucester and Maidstone to speak at Wings for Victory events. These were special events run by the National Savings organisation to encourage people to save money and thereby combat inflation. According to Angus Calder the propaganda for the schemes was actually 'economic nonsense' since financial institutions always issued bonds which made it quite easy for local committees to meet the monstrous targets that were set them. However, local Wings For Victory Weeks helped to raise morale and made people think that they were directly helping the war effort. So it was that the climax of Gibson's speech during Maidstone's Wings for Victory Week on Saturday 19 June was marked by the sight of four Lancasters, piloted by David Maltby, David Shannon, Micky Martin and Les Munro, 'beating up' the town.

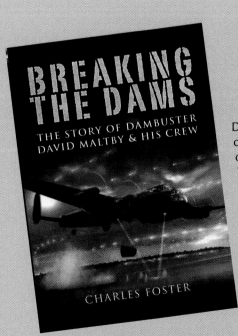

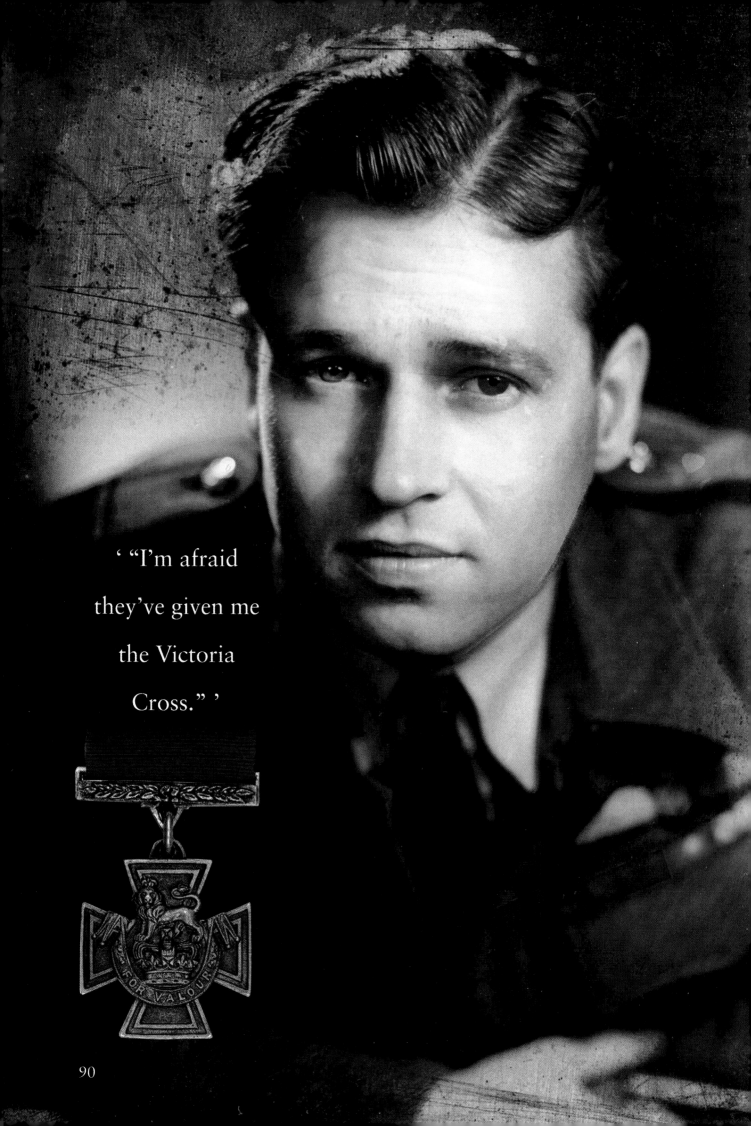

' "I'm afraid they've given me the Victoria Cross." '

FOR VALOUR

At 0725 on the morning of Monday 17 May 1943, a Spitfire XI EN343 of 542 Squadron took off from the home of photographic reconnaissance, RAF Benson in Oxfordshire. Its pilot was Flying Officer F G Fray. Three hours and thirty-five minutes later he returned to Benson having taken what is probably on of the most famous photographs of the war: that of the breached Möhne dam.

By Susan Ottaway

This article was extracted from *Dambuster - A Life of Guy Gibson VC* and is reproduced here by permission of Pen and Sword Books Ltd.

The film was rushed to the photographic interpretation unit at nearby RAF Medmenham and from there to No 5 Group headquarters at Grantham. The RAF made good use of this photograph and of the earlier photographs taken by Flying Officer Fray when they produced leaflets describing the operation and dropped them over the occupied European countries. For his part in the operation, Flying Officer Fray was awarded the DFC.

On 18 May the men of 617 Squadron were given special leave; three days for the ground crews and seven days for the aircrew. For Guy, however, the work was not yet complete. For three days he sat in his office, overlooking the grave of his beloved friend. Nigger, and wrote letters to the families of those who had not returned. Each letter contained something different, something personal, and by the time he had completed the 56 letters he was physically and emotionally exhausted. Although he kept his feelings tightly under control, the loss of so many men affected him deeply. These were the boys with whom he had flown. They had lived side by side for the past two months, sharing a joke or the odd drink in the Mess and now they were gone. He knew it was not his fault and that an operation like this was bound to produce heavy casualties, but, nonetheless, they were his men and he felt responsible for them. The last thing he could do for them was to inform their families in a personal, sensitive way.

Eve Gibson thought that her husband had been grounded. That is what he had told her and she had no reason to believe anything different. Since she lived in

Sir Archibald Sinclair.

Sir Trafford Leigh-Mallory

London she had no way of knowing what Guy was doing on a day-to-day basis. She was, therefore, amazed when a friend told her what she had just heard on the wireless about the raid on the Ruhr dams.

Soon she was able to see for herself the reports that began appearing in the newspapers. Headlines such as; 'DAMS WERE BURST BY ONLY NINETEEN LANCASTERS', '60 MILES OF FLOOD IN RUHR VALLEY' and 'LANCASTER ACE SMASHED HITLER'S RUHR DAMS' were commonplace in the first few days after the raid. In a few more days she herself would be interviewed by newspaper reporters and would coyly tell them,

'I thought my husband was pen-pushing. He never talks about his work.'

Back at No 5 Group headquarters telegrams were coming in from, among others, Fighter Command, Coastal Command and the Secretary of State for Air, Sir Archibald Sinclair. Sir Archibald said in a lengthy message that

'The thorough tactical planning, the energy and drive behind the special preparation and, finally, the determined execution of this operation have combined to deal a grievous blow to the enemy and are worthy of the highest praise.'

In his very brief message AOC-in-C Coastal Command, Sir John Slessor, said;

'Well done 5 Group and Scampton. A magnificent night's work.'

The AOC-in-C Fighter Command, Sir Trafford Leigh-Mallory, was more effusive in his praise:

'Heartiest congratulations from all in Fighter

Command on your magnificent exploit in wrecking the Möhne and Eder dams. Probably the greatest and most far-reaching destruction yet wreaked on Germany in a single night.'

The Germans themselves had to admit that the raid had caused a considerable amount of damage. It took 5000 men four-and-a-half months to repair the damage to the Möhne and Eder dams, and the effects of the damage to the latter were still being felt as late as 1988 when it was discovered that the dam had moved several centimetres. In 1991 the site of the breach was, once again, being repaired.

There were other messages of praise, official and otherwise, not only for the Squadron but for the many other people involved in the entire operation. Barnes Wallis received a letter from Guy telling him how honoured he and his pilots were to have been part of the great experiment. He also said that Barnes Wallis had earned the thanks of the civilized world and went on to suggest that a holiday would be in order.

Guy himself was, by now, ready for a short break. Having completed his immediate post-raid duties, he went, with Eve, to spend a long weekend with his in-laws in Penarth. Whilst visiting a club in Cardiff on 22 May, Guy ran into another old boy of St Edward's School, Surgeon-Captain Stewart Goss, RN. Captain Goss was so impressed with Guy that on 24 May he wrote to the secretary of the St Edward's School society and gave his impressions of the meeting and his permission to quote from his letter in the School Chronicle, should he so desire. He said he had never met, in all his years of service, a more modest, charming, unspoilt and gallant lad but that it was only what he expected of an old boy of St Edward's.

The morning after Guy's meeting with Captain Goss he received a telephone call, at his in-laws' house, from Sir Arthur Harris informing him that he had been awarded the Victoria Cross. After replacing the receiver he stood in silence for a few moments, taking in the

news. He was, of course, delighted, but could not help thinking of all the men lost on the raid and told Eve that it seemed unfair somehow. Later on that afternoon Guy telephoned his aunt and uncle and told them, rather apologetically,

'I'm afraid they've given me the Victoria Cross.'

Many more letters of praise flooded in, although not all of them came directly to Guy. The Rev Kendall, Warden of St Edward's School, received many letters of congratulation from old boys and their relatives and friends. One letter informed Warden Kendall *'You will be doubly interested to know that my David was on the raid and that he has been given the DSO,'* and was signed Ettrick Maltby. All the correspondents were extremely proud that one of their own should have been so honoured.

Warden Kendall wrote, offering his own good wishes to Guy on the success of the raid and received a reply, dated 25 May, in which Guy added *'PS Was awarded VC yesterday.'* Guy wrote again on 30 May in reply to the Warden's letter of congratulation upon the award of his VC. He began by saying that he thought that the stuff which had appeared in the papers was *'pretty good tripe'* and closed with;

'All the "old boys" have done wonderfully, and it is to those who have fallen, I think, that we ought to raise our glasses.'

At the end of May, King George VI and Queen Elizabeth began a 500-mile, two-day tour of seven RAF stations and two US Army Air Corps bases. During a visit to one of the latter they had been shown a B17 Flying Fortress, the Memphis Belle which, with its crew, had just completed its twenty-fifth daylight raid. Twenty-five missions was a record for the Americans and the crew, shortly after meeting the Royal visitors, were sent home as heroes. A film, directed by William Wyler, was made about the Memphis Belle and her crew. On 27 May the

> 'All the "old boys" have done wonderfully, and it is to those who have fallen, I think, that we ought to raise our glasses.'

The jubilant crew of the Memphis Belle, running towards the camera after completing and surviving 25 daylight missions. Like Guy Gibson and other 617 Squadron members, they were to return home to a hero's welcome.

H M The King meeting the ground crews of 617 Squadron. Second from the right is the Squadron Armament Officer, Harry 'Doc' Watson.

the use of the models of the dams and the King was very interested in what he had to say and asked several questions.

Curiously enough Guy had, upon learning of His Majesty's visit, taken advice as to how much information he could impart to the royal visitors. Even with the raid over Guy was still very concerned with the security of the operation and was not prepared to disclose details to anyone, not even his King, without first obtaining permission.

During the Royal visit Guy showed the King two drafts of proposed badges for 617 Squadron. The first showed a hammer parting chains which were attached to a figure representing Europe. The motto beneath was 'Alter the Map.' The second, which was the one ultimately chosen, shows a breached dam with the motto 'Après moi le deluge' and symbols of lightning above the dam.

Much has been written in the years following the raid on the Ruhr dams about the actual effect it had on the German war effort. It has been said that although it took thousands of men months to clear up and repair the devastation, the damage caused by the raid was not sufficient to warrant the loss of so many aircrew. Others strenuously defend the operation, claiming that it was entirely justified. One fact cannot be disputed. The war had been a part of everyday life for three and a half years. People were weary and needed something to lift their spirits. As a morale booster the raid was second to none, not just for the British people but for their allies as well. People as far apart as America and Russia celebrated when they heard the news of the breaching of the dams. The authorities were quick to realize that this boost could be extended, long after the floods had subsided, by

Royal couple made a lunchtime visit to Scampton and met the men of 617 Squadron who were, by this time, being referred to as 'dambusters'. Guy was, of course, introduced to them both and he accompanied the King on his tour of inspection. Each crew was lined up in a separate group and the royal visitors made their way down the lines, meeting the men who had survived the raid. Cameras were very much in evidence and the visit was captured for posterity by *Gaumont British News* with an item entitled 'King visits the Dambusters'. As the newsreel begins. Guy is seen standing stiffly to attention, blinking in the sunlight. He looks very smart, more so than usual, and has obviously just been under the barber's scissors. His haircut is so severe that in some shots he appears almost bald.

After speaking to the men, which included the ground crews, the King can be seen walking back towards the buildings, accompanied by Guy with his rolling gait, almost like that of a sailor. Having reached the offices once more. Guy is seen explaining to the King how the squadron carried out the attack. His explanation was assisted by

Guy explaining to the King how the squadron carried out the attack. Due to the Royal visit, Guy sought advice on how much information he was allowed to impart to His Majesty.

Guy making an inspection during one of his visits.

calling attention to the crews who had taken part and, more especially, to the leader of the operation.

Guy, therefore, found he had become a celebrity almost overnight. Even before the award of his Victoria Cross had been announced, he was in demand for appearances at fund-raising activities. The *Sheffield Telegraph* ran an article on 28 May advising its readers that the following day Sheffield would be privileged to welcome, not only Mrs Winston Churchill but also *'the man of the moment in the air war'* Wing Commander Guy Gibson. Guy arrived in Sheffield that evening and went directly to Riverdale Grange, Fulwood, where he was the guest of Lord and Lady Riverdale. A photo of Guy and his host and hostess appeared on the front page of the *Sheffield Telegraph* the next morning, Saturday, 29 May.

Before the start of the Wings Week parade Guy accompanied Mrs Churchill to a lunch given by the Lord Mayor at the City Hall. Here Guy was given a pocket knife of Sheffield steel by the chairman of the savings committee, Mr Ashley S Ward. In her speech marking the start of the fund-raising, Mrs Churchill introduced Guy and said that she was sure there was not any woman of her own age in the hall who would not be glad and proud if he were her son. These sentiments must have been especially poignant to Guy, given his background, but he smiled broadly while the audience gave him a standing ovation.

Guy began his speech by telling the assembled

company that he had been to Sheffield before but had not had such a welcome that time. He explained that his previous visit had been as a fighter pilot during December, 1940, when the city had suffered its worst bombing and said,

'I had the displeasure of watching your city burn and I knew then the time would come when we would do the same to them on a much bigger scale. We always say we Britons can take it, but we can also give it.'

He continued that Bomber Command was hammering the heart of Germany and that, if it continued to do so, the German people would soon be unable to take any more. He agreed with what Mrs Churchill had said about a bombing raid being more like a battle and compared the 6000 men which he said were sometimes involved in a single raid with the equivalent number of soldiers landing on the French coast. In his view that would definitely be regarded as a battle and he wanted people to realize that airmen were doing just as much as the soldiers to make their presence felt to the enemy. He stressed the need for more money to make more munitions and concluded by saying that he would like to see everyone, young and old alike, working to make the world a better place in which to live, once peace had been achieved.

Less than two weeks after the raid Guy was standing on the saluting base with Mrs Churchill, Air

'We always say we Britons can take it, but we can also give it.'

Guy and Eve Gibson after the investiture at Buckingham Palace on 22 June 1943.

Commodore J G Murray and the Lord Mayor of Sheffield, Councillor H E Bridgwater, taking the salute as the parade passed in front of a crowd of over 3000. It was a position which, a few months before, he would never have imagined would be his fate. He tackled this new role, however, with characteristic enthusiasm and thoroughness and did not seem at all fazed by the crowds and the attention he was receiving.

Even after Guy had left Sheffield and gone on to London to receive his Victoria Cross, stories were still appearing in the Sheffield newspapers about him. A report on 1 June told a story of the superintendant of Sheffield town hall, Mr E A Beasley. This gentleman had watched the blitz in 1940 from a balcony in the town hall tower. He saw not only German bombers, but also two British fighters, but when he told his story no one believed that there were any British planes about that night. Having heard in Guy's speech that he had flown over Sheffield and seen it burn Mr Beasley felt his story must now be accepted. An unimportant little story perhaps, but it does illustrate how the media were making good use of every column inch they could squeeze from the newest holder of the Victoria Cross.

On 25 May the *Maidstone Gazette* announced that Guy would be taking part in their 'Wings for Victory' Week to be held in June. They were also at pains to point out that, although Guy was not a Kent man by birth, he did have strong links with the county, having been educated in Folkestone.

For Guy the trip down to Maidstone gave him the chance to renew old friendships. Group Captain Colbeck-Welch had also been invited to take part in the Wings week, as had Guy's old scouting friend, Glad Bincham.

The week of activities began on Saturday, 19 June with a lunch at The Royal Star hotel and continued with a grand parade. Guy watched as the crowds were treated to a flypast of three Lancasters. The aircraft were piloted by Micky Martin, David Maltby and Dave Shannon and the display was rather unusual in that the three aircraft were flying on only six of their twelve engines. Micky Martin led the flight using his two inner engines. On his left was David Maltby flying on his two port and on his right was David Shannon using his two starboard engines. The following evening The Royal Star was the venue for an auction conducted by comedian Richard Hearne. Guy had been billed to assist the 'auctioneer' but remained in the audience, claiming it was against King's Regulations to take part in such an event. This prompted the comment from Richard Hearne,

'I understood that Wing Commander Gibson was going to help me with the sale, but I am glad he is not. He would probably have made an awful mess of it. Look what he did to the Ruhr!'

In spite of Guy's lack of assistance, the auction was a success and raised £4800. The largest single sum was £1000 paid for two bottles of whisky, a bottle of gin and a bottle of sherry which had been donated by Glad Bincham. Guy donated a bottle of Liebfraumilch, which he autographed and this was sold, along with six rolls of wallpaper, for £600!

Earlier that day Guy had been to visit the 1st Tovil troop where Glad was scoutmaster. Guy had been a scout as a boy and had expressed a desire to 're-muster' as he put it, as a Rover scout. This he did that afternoon along with Group Captain E Colbeck-Welch, DFC, Wing Commander S P Richards, AFC, Flight Lieutenant K Davison and Lieutenant F Carruthers, RA. He spoke afterwards of his time in the scouts as a boy and admitted that the only badge he had attempted was the cook's badge. He also told the scout troop that his membership of the movement had taught him the decent things in life – resourcefulness, courage and devotion to duty.

When he spoke a little later in London at the Boy Scout Association's annual meeting he said,

'I, for one, hope we are not going to be too lenient with the Germans after the war. The young super goose-stepping Nazi brought up to

'I understood that Wing Commander Gibson was going to help me with the sale, but I am glad he is not. He would probably have made an awful mess of it. Look what he did to the Ruhr!'

Guy poses for the press alongside his comrades outside Buckingham Palace.

the Nazi creed from the age of three, who hates everything except arrogance and cruelty, is going to be hard to re-educate. It will take much washing to make him clean.'

Two days after re-joining the Scouts, Guy was once again at a ceremony, this time at Buckingham Palace where he collected a bar to his DSO, and the Victoria Cross.

The citation for the award of the Victoria Cross was quite long and detailed Guy's career up to date. It spoke of his outstandingly successful results, both as a pilot and as a leader, and stated that his courage knew no bounds. With regard to the raid on the Ruhr dams for which Guy had received the award, the citation said:

'Under his inspiring leadership this squadron has now executed one of the most devastating attacks of the war – the breaching of the Möhne and Eder dams. The task was fraught with danger and difficulty. Wing Commander Gibson personally made the initial attack on the Möhne dam. Descending to within a few feet of the water and taking the full brunt of the anti-aircraft defences, he launched his projectiles with great accuracy. Afterwards he circled very low for thirty minutes, drawing the enemy fire on himself in order to leave as free a run as possible to the following aircraft which were attacking the dam in turn.'

The citation continued with a completely inaccurate statement that Guy had used the same decoy tactics at the Eder dam and then concluded:

'Wing Commander Gibson has completed

'At the age of 24, Guy Gibson had become the most highly decorated man of the entire war.'

over 170 sorties, involving more than 600 hours operational flying. Throughout his operational career, prolonged exceptionally at his own request, he has shown leadership, determination and valour of the highest order.'

Eve Gibson accompanied her husband to Buckingham Palace, the fourth time she had made such a trip. As the King was on a visit to the troops in North Africa, the investiture was conducted by the Queen. Her own standard flew over the Palace on the morning of 22 June and she stood alone, in a grey costume trimmed with pink orchids, as she presented the awards to 617 Squadron and over 200 others.

Guy received his two awards first, followed by the other members of his Squadron in alphabetical order. The Queen chatted to all the recipients, remembering many of their names from her visit to Scampton the previous month. Eve, sitting close to the front, strained her ears to hear what the Queen was saying to Guy but was unsuccessful.

Outside the Palace the press was waiting to pounce. Photographs were taken and another newsreel captured Guy proudly marching, with his Squadron around him. As soon as he was able. Guy escaped back to his hotel room where he was interviewed by a *Daily Mirror* reporter who said in his article that the man who had braved the raid on the dams was afraid to face the crowds waiting to welcome him outside the Palace. Guy did admit that he was glad it was all over. His relief was more due to tiredness than to fear of the crowds. Since the middle of May he had done little else but face large crowds and was becoming quite used to being regarded as a celebrity.

At the age of 24, Guy Gibson had become the most highly decorated man of the entire war. The neglected little boy with lofty ambitions had surpassed even his own expectations. He had made a success of his life, in spite of all the problems of his youth. Who could blame him for feeling proud of his achievements?

On the evening of the investiture a party was given by A V Roe and Co at the Hungaria restaurant in London's Lower Regent Street. Many, but not all, 617 Squadron members were present. They had mostly travelled down together by train from Lincolnshire, and the atmosphere during the journey was that of a party. The silly tricks usually reserved for the Mess were performed on the train, leaving the other passengers to wonder what on earth was happening. After the ceremony at Buckingham Palace some of them went off to celebrations of their own. Others had intended to attend the party but had been detained by their families and friends or by well-wishers in the pubs to which some of them had retired. It was said that in the days after the raid no member of 617 Squadron was permitted to pay for anything whilst in London – drinks, taxi rides, all were provided free. Those who were present at the party received a menu card on which they were described as 'Damn Busters.' This was discovered later not to be a deliberate pun but rather the work of someone who was very bad at spelling. The cards were put to good use during the evening, however, being used to collect the autographs of the many distinguished guests, who included Roy Chadwick, designer of the Lancaster who had been given the CBE, and Barnes Wallis. Mr Chadwick said at the party that he was very proud to have been decorated with the boys of 617.

During the course of the evening, an enlarged copy of the photograph taken by Flying Officer Fray was autographed by the Squadron members present and was presented to Barnes Wallis. It was later to adorn a wall in his office.

Guy was presented with a silver model of a Lancaster by A V Roe's director Mr T Sopwith, who also placed the highest bid in the auction which was held that evening, for a fusing link from the first bomb to be dropped on the dams. This item raised £30 and the proceeds went to the RAF Benevolent Fund. Guy was asked to make a speech during which he said,

> *'Well, chaps, we have had a lot of praise, but this raid was not carried out by one man. It was carried out by a lot of people working hard.'*

Then he and the other aircrew raised their glasses to the ground crews present and sang;

> *'For they are jolly good fellows'.*

Life for the 'Dambusters' gradually got back to normal. They returned to Scampton where some continued with 617 Squadron while others were posted. Guy did not fly again following the raid until the beginning of July as he was still busy in his public relations role.

The workers at the aircraft factories were not forgotten and Guy, with some of his crews, visited the A V Roe works at Chadderton to talk to and thank the people who had built the Lancaster bomber. As a souvenir of the visit, postcards were produced which showed a Lancaster in flight surrounded by the signatures of Guy and the other officers. These were sold for 6d in aid of war funds.

Guy and Eve Gibson carrying on with celebrations along with US Air Force men.

'Well, chaps, we have had a lot of praise, but this raid was not carried out by one man. It was carried out by a lot of people working hard.'

Visits to other establishments followed and Guy was often asked to say a few words. He was even booked to give talks to various groups, including the Women's Institute. At one such event, now quite well known, Guy was introduced to the ladies by the chairwoman. She was quite flustered at having such a famous guest speaker and introduced him as *'Wing Commander Gibson, the famous bomb duster.'* Guy was very amused by this slip and pulled a handkerchief from his pocket and pretended to dust, much to the delight of the ladies present.

On 12 July he made a visit to the Trent Lane headquarters of the ATC in Nottingham. Here he presented the Captain Albert Ball Victoria Cross Sword of Honour to Flight Sergeant Penniston. This was an especially proud moment for Guy, as Albert Ball had been his childhood hero. At the end of July Guy was invited, along with Eve, to spend the day with Winston Churchill at Chequers. When they arrived they were greeted by the Prime Minister who immediately whisked Guy off to the garden to help him with one of his building projects. The luncheon party consisted of eight men, Mrs Churchill and Eve. During the afternoon Guy's hatred of the Nazi system was reinforced when he and Eve were shown a film which had, somehow, been brought from Germany and showed the atrocities being committed at Hitler's concentration camps. Before the couple left Chequers, Mr Churchill hinted that he had plans to extend Guy's public relations role, possibly to include a trip overseas.

RESULTS OF THE RAID ON THE DAMS 16-17 MAY 1943

Damage caused to the Ruhr Valley by breaching of Möhne Dam.

Factories destroyed	11
Factories damaged	114
Bridges destroyed	25
Bridges damaged	21
Power stations destroyed/damaged	9
Water pumping stations affected	15
Houses/Farms destroyed	92
Houses/Farms badly damaged	1003
German dead	476
German missing	69
Foreign dead	593
Foreign missing	156
Cattle and pigs dead	6316

The foreign dead and missing were the inmates of a labour camp situated at Neheim, where the River Möhne joins the River Ruhr. They included 439 Ukrainian women as well as French and Belgian prisoners of war and Dutch male labourers.

The water was 30 feet deep and fast flowing. Many kilometres of roads were washed away and 4000 hectares of farmland were rendered useless.

Damage caused to Eder Valley by breaching of Eder Dam.

Workplaces destroyed/damaged	101
Bridges destroyed	14
Power stations out of action	4
Houses destroyed/damaged	112
German dead	47
Cattle and pigs dead	very many

The military airfield at Fritzlar and large proportion of the industrial area of Kassel were flooded and severely damaged. Several thousand hectares of arable land were rendered useless.